Carrying
the Cross
to
Columbine

Carrying the Cross to Columbine

by
Garlin Newton

THE COLBERT HOUSE
NORMAN, OKLAHOMA

Unless otherwise noted, Scripture quotations are from the New King James Version of the Bible.

ISBN: 1-887399-06-2

Printed in the United States of America

Cover design: Shawn Hancock

PUBLISHED BY
THE COLBERT HOUSE
NORMAN, OKLAHOMA

We are filling the earth
with the knowledge of the glory of Jesus Christ.

CONTENTS

ACKNOWLEDGMENTS

I'd like to thank several people and organizations for their help during my walk to Columbine High School.

The people who supported me especially are: my mother Roberta Craig, my daughters Ammie Timms and Windie Meeks, my son-in-law David, and my grandson Colby. Youth pastor Jason Janz at South Sheraton Baptist Church in Littleton, Colorado, gave the Bernall family a Bible for me and Steve Schweitzberger showed me particular kindness. Thanks to Dad, Garlin Newton, Sr., who took care of my stables while we were gone. It would not have been possible without him. I appreciate my brother-in-law and good friend Carroll Jordan for moral and spiritual support.

I thank Pastor David Ford and his wife Rebecca of St. John Baptist Church in St. John, Kansas; also my pastor Ron Gadberry at Christian Faith Church in Edmond, Oklahoma; and in Colorado, KOA Campgrounds in Lamar and Kiowa Fair-grounds in Kiowa.

Elaine Balkan of Balkan Siding in Oklahoma City gave financially in support of my journey to Columbine; Baker's Signs in El Reno donated the signs for the cross and our truck; and Jerry Merrell with All American Building Products gave us the material to build the cross. Thanks to Larry Colbert for his help and guidance with this book. He was truly sent by God to help me with it.

The *Edmond Sun*, *Garden City Telegram*, the *Denver Post*, *Lamar Daily News*, TBN Channel 14 in Oklahoma City, and the Tulsa-based Oasis Radio Network showed special kindness to me.

DEDICATION

I dedicate *Carrying the Cross to Columbine* to my wife Lori. She was all that she could be and all that I needed as I tried to follow the Lord's direction. She never wavered and always encouraged me. I love her deeply, and without her I would never have been able to carry the cross to Columbine High School.

Thank you, Lori.

Chapter One
The Call to Carry the Cross

It all happens after prayer.

The signature statement of Jesse Woodfork, late pastor,
Community Missionary Baptist Church,
Norman, Oklahoma

What man in his right mind would carry a cross 700 miles to encourage Christian prayer in public schools? The answer is a man who had no children in school, who belonged to no activist group, who supported his family with two small businesses, and who had given his life to Christ only ten months before.

I am that man. I am Garlin Newton and my story began on a day that was much like any other day in my life—*before God interrupted me.*

Owner of Sooner Home Improvement since 1981, I had been putting siding on a room addition in El Reno, a town of 15,000 people a few miles west of Oklahoma City. One morning as I drove to work down Interstate 40, I saw for a split second a man in blue jeans carrying a white cross. It was like a video clip overlaying the highway. I couldn't see his face; I only saw his back. I couldn't tell what highway he was on nor where he was going. I could see the wide shoulder of the highway, the white lines, and the green mile marker.

It looked so real that as I drove past I glanced in my rearview mirror to get a better look at him, but he was gone. All of a sudden I wasn't sure what I had seen or if I had seen anything at all.

It was as though a daydream had occurred in front of my eyes, and I tried to make some sense of it. When I was eight years old on a trip to California with my parents, I had seen a man carrying a cross on Route 66 and watched him out of the rear window after we drove by. What the man looked like had long since passed from my memory, but he had made an impression on me, and I wondered if what I had seen was an exceptional flashback of that man. Or had I simply gone batty?

For a few moments I thought about telling somebody what I had seen *or thought I had seen*, but I was afraid they would think I was crazy. Two days later I still hadn't been able to put the incident out of my mind. It had seemed so real, but I knew it wasn't.

Then it happened again.

As I drove home from El Reno after work, I saw the man carrying a cross. It was exactly like the first time, sort of like a video clip: he was on my side of the road and dressed in blue jeans, and I only saw his back. When I looked in my rearview mirror, he was gone.

I wondered what was going on. Had I been thinking about the first time so much that I imagined this second incident? Was something really wrong with my mind, or was I just tired? I had been working ten to twelve hours a day, six days a week, but that was not unusual for me. Nothing like this had ever happened to me before, and I was beginning to get concerned.

I was still fearful of what others would think and didn't tell anybody about the second incident. I had good reason. Just after I gave my life to the Lord, I lost several friends who thought I was crazy for accepting Christ, and some of my other friends didn't like being around me anymore. I didn't want to lose them, too, and telling them something like that would surely run them off.

I didn't even tell my wife Lori. I didn't want her to think I'd gone crazy either. But I did begin wondering if I had seen a vision. I had heard about visions only briefly and had read in

the Bible about people having them. At one point I looked up
Joel 2:28:

> *And it shall come to pass afterward*
> *That I will pour out My Spirit on all flesh;*
> *Your sons and your daughters shall prophesy,*
> *Your old men shall dream dreams,*
> *Your young men shall see visions.*

Understanding that seeing visions was scriptural, I didn't
doubt their realness. What I doubted was that God would give
me one.

I also own stables, and several days later, as I hauled an old
horse out of town, I again saw the man carrying the cross beside
the road. This time I knew it wasn't a daydream or anything
else. This time it was as clear as anything that I had every seen,
and I saw it for three seconds or more. The man was wearing a
brown robe and was carrying a white cross with a white sign on
the back, which said in big, bright red capital letters, "GOD
WANTS PRAYER BACK IN SCHOOL."

But I could also see something else this time. I could identify
the man carrying the cross. That man was me!

I understood that God was telling me through this vision to
carry a cross. Tears of joy started flowing down my cheeks, and
I didn't think they were ever going to stop.

Shocked that I had seen a vision and excited to discover that
God wanted to use me, I didn't think a lot about the message on
the sign. Yet it is the message of the need for prayer in schools
that has become a major force in my life.

God was going to use *me*. After I had gotten saved, I began listening to the Bible on cassette eight to ten hours a day while I
worked. As my love for Jesus grew, I started seeing how God
used people to help others, and I wanted to be a part of it. I started
ending my prayers by asking the Lord to use me any way He
wanted to. God's call for me to carry the cross was the answer to
my prayers.

I don't know why God picked me to carry a cross. Born in Shawnee, Oklahoma, I have lived in Oklahoma City most of my life and always worked with my hands. I have been married more than twenty-five years, have one stepdaughter, Tonya Potts, and two daughters, Windie Meeks and Ammie Timms. I started working with siding when I was a preteen and spent three years in the Army. None of my immediate family was a Christian. Then, in 1998, Keith Henley, pastor of Trinity Baptist Church in El Reno, led me to the Lord while I was working on a siding job.

God's choice of me to carry a cross is even more mysterious because when He called me, I had worn knee braces for seven years and took four to twelve pain pills a day for them. I also had hernias in both groins.

I'm not anybody special whom God would trust to pass on His message. But He's the one who chose a childless man to become the father of many nations and picked a boy to fight a giant and become a king even though his own father thought he was unimportant. Carrying a cross doesn't compare with what Abraham or David did. But I was just glad to be chosen. God does the choosing, the Word says in Isaiah and John:

> *Also I heard the voice of the Lord, saying:*
> *"Whom shall I send,*
> *And who will go for Us?"*
> *Then I said, "Here am I! Send me."* (Isa. 6:8)

> *You did not choose Me, but I chose you and appointed you that you should go and bear fruit, and that your fruit should remain, that whatever you ask the Father in My name He may give you.* (John 15:16)

I knew I had to put myself in God's hands to carry a cross. I heard a preacher say once that God does not choose the prepared; He prepares the chosen. I expected God to prepare me to carry it.

At this point I didn't know when or where I would carry a cross. I felt God would let me know, and I decided not to tell anyone until I knew more about what I was to do.

On the morning of April 20, 1999, my one-year anniversary of being a Christian, I was driving to a siding job when the radio reported the shooting at Columbine High School in Littleton, Colorado. In that terrible event, two high school students killed twelve of their classmates and a teacher, destroyed property with homemade bombs and by setting fires, and then committed suicide. Several students and teachers were injured. The massacre shook up Columbine High School, the community, and the whole nation.

When I heard the news, it seemed like I went into shock. I just couldn't believe it, and tears started flowing down my cheeks. I was crying so hard that I could barely see to drive. As I started praying for the students and their families, the Holy Spirit spoke to me: "Carry the cross from Oklahoma City to Purcell."

I was excited. Now I had a destination, Purcell, a town of fewer than 5,000 people about thirty miles south of Oklahoma City.

On the one hand this was good news, but on the other hand it meant that I had to tell people God wanted me to carry a cross. I suspected that when I did people would ridicule and make fun of me. I didn't look forward to any of that, but as long as my wife and family stood behind me, I felt I could take it.

I understood that the cross would bear the sign, "GOD WANTS PRAYER BACK IN SCHOOL," but I still didn't give a lot of thought to it. Of course we had prayed regularly when I was in school until I entered the seventh grade. None of my relatives or friends talked about God, so school was where I found out that He existed.

At this time my single-minded goal was to obey God. He was going to use me and I wasn't about to let Him down. I had no idea then that I would carry a cross 700 miles. I had even less idea how God would mature me as a Christian and how He would use me to minister to people I met on the highway.

When I recorded what happened on my way to Columbine High School, I never meant to use the tapes to write a book. I only made them for my wife and myself as a record of what I experienced, felt, and thought during the walk. The idea to write a book came several months later.

In this book, *Carrying the Cross to Columbine,* I will share how I tried to obey God in this new direction of my life and the many instances of God's care that I saw and experienced on my walks, especially on the journey to Columbine High School. I didn't see the dead raised or limbs growing out, but I did see what Scripture calls "a more excellent way," products of God's love from the human heart.

I hope you'll enjoy reading *Carrying the Cross to Columbine.*

Chapter Two
Preparation to Carry the Cross

Now when He had taken the scroll, the four living creatures and the twenty-four elders fell down before the Lamb, each having a harp, and golden bowls full of incense, which are the prayers of the saints.

Revelation 5:8

I decided to carry the cross to Purcell on May 1, less than two weeks after the Columbine tragedy. I didn't know why God wanted me to carry it to Purcell, but I had to quickly make the cross, route the walk, and contact the minister at Purcell Assembly of God church, the destination I had chosen.

The first person I decided to tell I was going to carry a cross was my brother-in-law and close friend Carroll Jordan, but I didn't know how to tell him without sounding crazy. A dark haired, gentle hearted man, Carroll sometimes worked with me on siding jobs.

While we were in a restaurant talking about the Columbine shooting, I tried to feel Carroll out before I told him. I asked him, "Why don't you do something about that?"

"Why don't *you* do something about it?" he replied.

I tried to get the words out but I couldn't tell him right then. Perhaps, I thought, I was too new with Christ to be doing something so unusual and needed to settle it in my own head that I had heard from God before I could tell anybody. So I said, "Well, I'll figure something out and tell you." The truth was that I knew I had heard from God and that carrying the cross was important.

At about noon that day I got the nerve.

"Carroll," I said, "I'm going to carry a cross to Purcell."

He hesitated a moment, looking at me curiously. "What?"

"The American Civil Liberties Union has an opinion about prayer in schools. School administrators and teachers have an opinion, and so does God. He wants people in schools to pray without restrictions. Maybe by carrying a cross and publicizing that God wants prayer back in school, others will get involved and return prayer to school. It might prevent the Columbine tragedy from happening somewhere else."

Carroll, who didn't look at me like I was crazy at all, said, "That's a fine idea. Somebody needs to do something. I'm glad you are."

Carroll had accepted it a lot better than I thought he would, which was good because my faith was fragile and I had to get ready quickly. It was little more than a week before my May 1 walk and I was working every day, which didn't leave me much time to prepare.

I had to tell Lori next and I really didn't know what her reaction would be. I had been a "redneck" forty-seven years of my life. I had left for work one day unsaved and come home saved and a completely changed man. Now, after being a Christian less than a year, I was about to do something *really* crazy. Was it too soon after accepting Christ? Was it too drastic a change? How would I tell her I had gotten a vision from God?

Later at home, as I worked up the courage to say the words, I thought about leaving a letter in the bathroom explaining what I was about to do before I went to work, but I didn't.

Lori was on the patio, and Carroll and I were sitting in my pickup. I had a four by four in the truck bed to make the cross and Lori saw it. Since I often did things around the house when I had wood in the truck, she thought I had a project in the works.

An energetic blond with green eyes, she nodded at the wood and asked me, "What are you going to do with that?"

"I'll tell you later."

"No," she insisted. "Tell me now."

My heart started beating fast. Backing the truck up, I said, "I'm going to build a cross and carry it to Purcell." I instantly felt relieved.

But she was frowning. "Do what?"

It was bad enough telling her once, but she was acting like she hadn't heard me or didn't quite understand what I had said and I had to tell her all over again. "I'm going to build a cross and carry it to Purcell."

Her eyes were like green fire. "I can't believe this! Have you lost your mind!"

It was the kind of reaction I had feared most, but she didn't throw a fit or try to kill me. I gunned the accelerator and got out of there. I hoped she wouldn't fight me over it.

Lori explained later what she thought after I told her. "I really was in shock the first few days and kept quiet about it, hoping it wasn't real. I had been around a lot of Christian people in my life, but not anyone who wanted to do something that extreme!"

This new direction in my life was almost too much for Lori to accept. A prodigal herself then, she had seen a change in me since I had accepted Christ and she wasn't sure how to take it.

She liked for me to build things around the house. "But after you got saved," she told me one day, "you listened to Bible tapes almost twenty-four hours a day, even while you were sleeping. Your language changed. You talked about how you loved God. It's like you went to bed one person and woke up another one. I thought you were out of touch with reality."

Lori's most serious concern about me walking was for my health. She asked God why He wanted to send me, since I had hernias and bad knees. She wondered how I could carry a cross when my knees hurt me day and night just with normal walking. "You already had an appointment to have surgery on the hernias," she said, "and if I thought I could have talked you out of walking until after your surgery, I would have.

"I just couldn't understand what was going on. Nevertheless, I didn't want to discourage your faith and after spending many hours praying, I was slowly assured that you had heard from God and that I should not question God's direction for you."

After I told Lori, I felt like I had to tell others that God wanted prayer back in school and that I was going to carry a cross to Purcell. I wanted my family and friends to be as excited as I was.

Then I started telling people. Surprise! Surprise! Many of them weren't excited at all!

Family members, friends, and Christians asked me if I thought I was Jesus Christ and accused me of wanting to carry a cross to build up my ego.

That hurt my feelings pretty badly. I don't even like walking, and carrying a cross thirty-some miles is a crazy way to get recognition. I knew I couldn't do it without bringing attention on myself, but I wasn't looking for any credit. I merely wanted to obey God.

At one point the pastor who had led me to Christ, Keith Henley, a large-framed man whose blue-gray eyes overpowered his light gray hair, sat me down in his office. Our talking wasn't unusual; we had become real friends in the time since I got saved. After pouring each of us a cup of coffee, Henley looked at me with affection and said, "Some people think they can jump off a cliff and the Lord will catch them before they hit bottom."

His meaning was quite clear to me. I hadn't told him about carrying the cross yet, but someone else had and evidently had asked him to talk to me. This didn't upset me much because a member of the congregation had recently committed suicide and Henley wanted to make sure I wasn't suffering mental problems.

With a smile, I said, "I'm right with God and I know what I'm doing. I'm not going to jump off a cliff."

That seemed to satisfy him, but my family (except for Lori, who had accepted what I was about to do by then) couldn't understand what was going on. Most of them only mentioned my carrying a cross once. They seemed to think Lori and I were crazy.

All the negative reactions were building up inside me. Then one person asked me if I thought I was a disciple of Christ, and I couldn't take any more. I was too young in Christ to handle the criticism alone. That afternoon when I got to my stables to feed the horses, I entered a stall and fell to my knees. I cried like a baby. "God," I said, "I can't understand these reactions, especially from Christians. Give me the strength I need not only for the walk but to forgive and to understand the things I need to."

As I walked out, the heavy weight lifted from my shoulders. I was overjoyed. I felt just like a thoroughbred, ready to run the race of my life! I felt new, fresh and excited like I had been saved all over again, as it says in 2 Corinthians 5:17:

Therefore, if anyone is in Christ, he is a new creation; old things have passed away; behold, all things have become new.

Although the reaction of many of my friends and family were negative, the Lord placed people who felt positive about me carrying a cross in my path to reassure me. One such person was Henley—after he was convinced I was okay. Since he had an investment in my salvation, I thought he had to hang in there with me! I called him often enough to make a nuisance of myself. Henley, however, gave me sound counsel and support, and told me how Jesus was laughed at and made fun of too in Luke 18:32:

For He will be delivered to the Gentiles and will be mocked and insulted and spit upon.

Those are not the most encouraging things a Christian could hear would happen to him, but I knew I was in good company!

As the day for my first walk drew near, Carroll and I charted a route down Interstate 35, starting from Moore, a few miles south of Oklahoma City. I had never walked that far at one time and figured it would take two days. Several days before the walk, we went to Purcell Assembly of God church. I didn't know their pastor, Duane Elmore, so I wasn't sure what to expect from him. I told him, "I'm going to carry a cross to your church. I will begin walking Saturday and arrive Sunday, in time for church services."

Elmore replied, "I'm excited about it. I'll be looking for you."

I was encouraged by his reaction when I left.

Another positive man who helped me was the associate pastor of Faith Tabernacle Church in Oklahoma City, Theodore Hughes, a slender-built, energetic African-American whom I had heard speak and had fallen in love with. Sitting at his desk when I told him that I would carry a cross to Purcell and why, Hughes shot to his feet.

He said, "I want to be a part of this! A soul might get saved because of it and be added to my account in heaven."

Hughes then prayed for me, and my faith strengthened even more.

A couple of days before I left for Purcell, I figured I had told everybody about it: strangers, my siding customers, and several churches. I had done everything in my power to get the word out.

I also got one mobile phone and Lori and Carroll got another so we could communicate while I was on the highway. I had borrowed one of the phones from my stepfather Jimmy Nye, who was unsaved.

The day I borrowed it, Nye told me, "There are a lot of people around who might hurt you while you're walking on the road."

I had already prayed about the danger, but I sensed a softness in his heart. His concern was a show of his love for me. I felt that the moment was from the Holy Spirit and an opportunity to witness to him. "If something happens to me on this walk and I don't make it," I said, "don't let it be in vain. Get to know the Lord."

Nye normally didn't show much emotion, but tears came to his eyes.

I knew he was behind me then. I appreciated it.

While preparations were still to be made and I was anxious and raring to go, I kept feeling God's presence. I was full of the Holy Spirit when I was working. I felt like I was floating on a cloud. When I heard people talk about the Lord on the radio while I was driving, I would pull over and start crying. It was probably one of the most Holy Spirit filled times of my life. I think I know what it feels like to be in heaven.

A day and a half before walking to Purcell, I was still full of the Holy Spirit. I had probably two hours worth of work to do, but it took me the full day and a half to do it.

I wanted Lori to share what I was feeling and to make sure that she would get through the walk all right. "Lord," I prayed, "fill Lori with the Holy Spirit. Reassure her. I've got to build the cross."

The Monday before I walked to Purcell, I built a cross at my stables out of two 4" x 4" cedar posts. It weighed about thirty-five pounds, which I didn't mind. I planned to paint it white as it was in my vision.

When my father saw it, he said, "That's going to be too heavy, son."

"Think so?"

"Yes."

Later that day Lori made a similar comment. "It's going to be pretty heavy, Garlin, and why does it have to be made out of cedar?"

I realized they were correct and remembered that hollow vinyl fence post would be much lighter, and I could purchase white posts.

I ordered the vinyl from All-American Building Products and it came in Friday morning before my walk. When I went to pick up the materials, Jerry Merrill, the owner and a long-time friend of mine, said, "No charge."

I protested, but Merrill said, "It's free. Take it."

That day I also picked up the sign, "GOD WANTS <u>PRAYER</u> BACK IN SCHOOL," which was made by Baker's Sign & Design. When I got there I found two signs instead of one. There was a lightweight durable vinyl real estate sign turned sideways and a magnetic sign with the same message for the tailgate of my pickup. Ryan Baker, owner of the company, said, "The signs are free. I've got children who go to school and I want prayer in schools again, too."

Because I had so much work to complete that day, it was 8:30 before I could make the cross. I took the two vinyl posts, tools, and two sawhorses to my dad's mobile home. It was already dark and I planned to make the cross, get home, and get a good night's sleep so I would be rested for the walk the next day. I set the sawhorses under the porch light my dad had turned on and plugged in an extension cord for other lights and my power tools.

As I got set up, Dad came out to help me. In my opinion, a son should never get too old for his father's help. I was forty-eight and Dad was seventy-four at that time and had had a stroke the previous year. He had been a sheet metal worker for years and knew how to use tools and take measurements.

First we laid one vinyl post on my shoulder at the angle I would carry the cross. With one end on the ground and the other resting on my shoulder, my dad marked where it naturally fell. We laid that on the sawhorse. Then we marked the other post at four feet, cut it and laid it crossways on the marked eight-foot piece. We notched and cut both pieces to fit and joined them.

It was perfect. Then I drilled two holes through both posts

where they fit, bolted the pieces together, and snapped caps on the ends.

Now the cross needed the sign and a wheel to keep me from dragging the cross on the pavement. Without the wheel, the road would literally eat the vinyl away.

For that, we made a fitting of two flat steel bars by drilling holes in each and bolting them together. To that we attached a lawn mower wheel. On the back of the cross, I screwed in the sign, "GOD WANTS PRAYER BACK IN SCHOOL."

The cross was ready!

Feeling pleased with our effort, I looked at my dad. "Thanks for helping me."

Tears formed in his blue eyes and started running down his cheeks.

"I'm leaving early in the morning, Dad, and won't see you until I get back from the walk."

"Good-bye, son."

As I picked up the cross and headed for the pickup, Dad wiped the tears from his eyes. When you love someone like Dad loved me, you don't have to say anything. I think helping me build the cross was Dad's way of saying he was behind me.

Now everything was ready, including me.

Chapter Three
Early Journeys

Now all things are of God, who has reconciled us to Himself through Jesus Christ, and has given us the ministry of reconciliation.
2 Corinthians 5:18

I drove to Moore, Oklahoma, and was ready to go at daybreak Saturday. With light wind and the temperature in the high sixties, the conditions were almost perfect. It was a beautiful May morning.

I felt better that day than I ever had. I seemed like I had the strength of Samson. God had told me to carry a cross and I was about to do it. I wanted to honor Him in every way I could.

Besides the cross, I carried two Bibles in a pouch to give to anybody who stopped me, which I actually didn't expect.

I looked out at four lanes of light Saturday morning traffic. Strips of businesses lined both sides of the highway and concrete barriers stood in the center.

Lori and Carroll were with me as I prayed: "Dear God, I ask You to give us the strength for what we are about to do. Sometimes we don't understand all the whys, but I know it is Your will for me to carry this cross to Purcell. We give You all of the praise and glory. May You watch over and guide us, in Jesus' name I pray, amen."

Dressed in a tan robe a lady had made for me and a camouflage brown bandanna tied to my head, I struck out for Purcell, walking south along Interstate 35.

While I really felt blessed out there carrying the cross on the highway for the first time, I thought I would feel like a gazing stock. But I was full of joy and excitement.

Lori and Carroll followed behind in the pickup, watching me. "You started off walking briskly, so fast that Carroll and I didn't believe what we were seeing," Lori told me later. "We even timed you; when you started out, you were moving at about five miles an hour."

I carried the cross a long ways, I thought, about eighteen miles, through the city of Norman and until I was about thirteen miles from Purcell. I was walking with the traffic, which was pretty loud.

"Hello, sir," someone behind me shouted.

I jumped slightly as I turned. A casually dressed, college-aged man with sandy, neatly cut hair walked toward me. I hadn't heard him approach because of the noise.

"Hello," I said and reached out my hand. I was surprised that he had stopped. Now, I had the idea that God wanted me to minister to people, and I thought, "I'm not a minister."

But God spoke to my heart, "Yes, you are. You have been a minister ever since you got saved."

Later, I got confirmation from the Word, in 2 Corinthians 5:18:

> *Now all things are of God, who has reconciled us to Himself through Jesus Christ, and has given us the ministry of reconciliation.*

And from Ephesians 3:7:

> *Of which I became a minister according to the gift of the grace of God given to me by the effective working of His power.*

"I drove past you," the man said, "and turned around to get to you."

When I realized the young man had driven several miles out of his way to talk with me, I was eager to hear why he had stopped.

"I read your sign," he said. He had a bottle of water in his hand and a big grin on his face.

"I'm glad you stopped."

As he handed me the water, his brown eyes lit up. "The Lord has blessed me so that I wanted to tell you to keep walking and telling people we need prayer in school."

"Thank you."

"I'm proud of you."

When the young man left, I was not only encouraged but also intrigued by the way God had used me. This young man's reaction to seeing the cross and the sign placed a whole new importance on the walk. What I thought might be the object of ridicule for me had turned out to be a reason to give Jesus honor and a moment of brotherly fellowship. We both had been blessed at the foot of the cross.

I walked a mile before a lady and her daughter, who looked eight years old, stopped and asked me if I was the person who had been on an area radio station talking about carrying a cross. I hadn't and told them so. After I explained my mission, the little girl gave me a five-dollar bill.

Choked up at her kindness, I pulled out a Bible, signed it, and gave it to her.

"Thank you and God bless you," the little girl said before they drove away.

As I picked up the cross, I was even more amazed that people were stopping and God was ministering to them and me. And I was enjoying it.

Lori and Carroll had gotten off on the service road and watched me through binoculars. "We followed farther back because when we were too close behind you, we blocked the view of the cross and the sign," she said later. "People stopped and talked when we were not too close, and I saw you wiping tears from your eyes a few times."

I hadn't traveled far before the Lord spoke to me. "If you carry the cross in during a Sunday church service," He said, "you will take eyes off Me and put them on yourself. You can make it today."

Wow! The wind had started blowing about forty miles an hour into my face and traffic had really picked up, including the eighteen-wheelers, which blew me sideways every time they went by. Carrying the cross and now fighting the strong winds and traffic made it a lot more difficult. Both knees had begun to ache. I wasn't bending them any longer and my pace had slowed down. But the Lord had said that I could walk the whole distance in one day. I hadn't thought I could make it.

I got Carroll on the phone and told him the new plan. We screamed to be heard over the howl of wind and traffic. A little later Lori and Carroll joined me for lunch. Perspiration soaked me to my waist and plastered my hair to my forehead. I was glad to lay the cross down for a few minutes. I could tell that Lori and Carroll had been crying. I had a fair idea neither of them thought I could make it.

While we sat in lawn chairs, I took off my shoes, socks, and knee braces so they could air out as we ate. When we finished, Lori washed my knees because salt from sweating had built up under the braces and would soon start irritating my skin.

She also rubbed Neosporin on two of my toes that were turning dark, put gauze pads between and round them, and bandaged them with a soft cloth-like tape to give them extra protection. It reminded me of Jesus washing the disciples' feet, demonstrating His love for them in a way many would call demeaning. I knew Lori hadn't been real sure about me doing this, but she had pitched in to help any way she could. I loved her for it and felt even more determined to finish that day.

"You're going to lose those toenails," she told me. "They're already turning black."

I looked at them and said, "Maybe." I powdered my knees, and put on the knee braces and two clean pair of socks. I then tied a towel to the cross so it wouldn't slip or rub my shoulder.

I started again and entered a hilly area a mile down the road.

The cross felt heavier and my legs were like lead weights. I started up the first hill, hurting with each step and gritting my teeth.

Lori and Carroll were less than a block behind. Carroll got out and walked with me, which he had done several times that day. "Your knees have bowed," he said. "Your ankles are almost touching the pavement."

And they're hurting up a storm too, I could have said. Every step had taken on its own individual struggle. I was dog tired. But I didn't want Lori any more upset than she was already and the pain really didn't matter. The Lord had said that I could finish the walk today and I would.

"You're not smiling anymore. Are you too tired to talk?"

I grinned at him. "Is Lori okay?"

"Yes."

"Good. I'll be through shortly."

Carroll stopped walking then and got back in the truck.

About that time I jumped up in the air and kicked my heels together to show Lori that I felt good.

I learned later that Lori wasn't convinced. She told me, "I couldn't stand watching you any more. So we drove on ahead of you. I knew what you were doing when you kicked up your heels."

My shoulders were dragging, but when they drove by, I threw up my hand. Around 4:30 that day, I got to the edge of Purcell and took the road toward town. I had about a mile to go. Within that space eight to ten people were waiting on me, cheering me on, talking to me, and praising the Lord.

One lady smiled and said, "Thank you," and gave me a bottle of water.

Another lady who had three kids said, "My husband is a preacher in Norman. When I saw you walking through town, I wanted my children to see you carrying the cross."

She had driven thirty miles out of her way. She looked at her children and said, "Look what this man is doing for you."

After they had left, I hadn't gone far when a man in a blue Ford truck stopped and walked toward me. Tears flowed down his cheeks as he handed me a bottle of water. He said, "God bless you."

We hugged each other and I thanked him. Then he walked back to his truck. He was still crying. He was like my dad; he said a lot without saying anything.

Ahead, I saw Lori and Carroll in the parking lot of an ice cream store and beyond them the Purcell City Limits sign. The walk was almost over. I felt like I had done something good. A few people had gotten the message that God wanted prayer back in school.

When I topped the hill walking into Purcell, the hardest part of it was past. I stopped at the ice cream store to wash my face and hands, wet my head down, and drink a soda. That seemed to revive me. I got to Purcell Assembly of God, which sits on the corner of the street, around five that evening. It was a single story, dark brown brick church with gables and a very green lawn. I had been walking since sunrise, about twelve hours.

At the church, I told the preacher, "I made the trip."

Pastor Elmore grinned and hugged me. "Praise the Lord."

No news people were there to do stories and those who had watched me had gone.

I loaded the cross in the truck and took off the wet robe. As I drove back to Oklahoma City, my legs were so sore that I could hardly lift them to step on the pedals. When I got home, I told Dad we made it.

I took a long hot bath and Lori put cream on my blistered feet and my toes. My shoulders weren't burned but they were very sore from the weight of the cross, and my knees were aching, sore, jerking, and throbbing badly with pain. I very slowly laid my sore, aching body into bed.

I felt good about completing the walk, especially in one day. It was the hardest walk I had ever had. I found out that I wasn't prepared or in shape physically. Places hurt on me that I didn't know existed. But I had made it. I learned that I can do anything if God is in it and that He will have you do things that you think are impossible.

Jesus said to him, "If you can believe, all things are possible to him who believes." (Mark 9:23)

Although Lori was pleased that I had completed the walk, she didn't think she could watch me carry the cross again. "I was totally drained from being so tense watching you suffer," she told me later. "I will never forget that day. It was horrible! I had never seen you in that condition before and I never wanted to experience it again!"

Although Lori had me soak my feet at least once a day for a good week, I lost my right toenail four or five days after the walk. A toenail didn't seem like a lot to lose to obey the Lord and receive the reward of joy from ministering to people.

The Sunday after I walked, I went to Christian Faith Church in Edmond. Ron Gadberry, the pastor, a medium-built man with a beautiful head of silver hair, said, "By looking at you, I can tell you finished your walk."

"I did," I said. Then I jokingly added, "I could give a testimony about it."

"Good. Come on up and give one."

He had misunderstood me. He thought I had offered to give a testimony. I had never spoken to a group, and in school I had taken Fs rather than talk before a class.

"Come on," Pastor Gadberry said, waving me to the front.

I stood there for a moment. All the pains in my body were gone, leaving only fear. As though in a daze, I walked to the platform. "Brother Ron," I whispered, "walking to Purcell was easy. This is much harder."

I don't remember what I said. I do remember keeping my head down a lot and that my face felt hot the whole time I stood there and talked. It was the longest four minutes of my life!

I thought my mission work with the cross had ended, but three weeks after I walked to Purcell, I felt that I needed to carry the cross to Christian Faith Church in Edmond, fourteen miles north of my front door in Oklahoma City.

The night before I went, I told Lori about it, which was easier than telling her about the first trip, but I didn't tell anybody else. I didn't publicize this trip because I felt the Lord planned to use it to teach me a few things.

It was a Saturday and it rained until about 11 o'clock. After it stopped, I got the cross and started out. By this time I had purchased a different brand of shoes and hoped they would be better on my feet.

The blacktop road in front of my house goes all the way to Interstate 35. It's a hilly area with few houses and a lot of trees. My neighbor, a quarter of a mile down the road from me, brought his children out to watch me as I walked past their house. They stood at the edge of the porch until I walked out of sight. I got a little thrill from that.

The first people I met were two African-American men in their early twenties. Looking like gang members with their tattoos and bandannas, they were in a low rider with the little tires and chrome wire wheels. Their boom box was going when they passed by—and pointed at me. I kept on walking. Then they made a U-turn in the middle of the road, came back, and stopped beside me. I wasn't sure what was about to happen.

"What are you doing?" one of them asked. Both men were frowning.

"I'm carrying this cross to Christian Faith Church in Edmond to promote getting prayer back in school."

They nodded as though they understood and that must have settled their curiosity.

"Will you come pray for our grandmother?" one of them asked. "She's sick."

"Sure," I said and gave them my business card. "Call me around seven tonight and I'll come pray for her."

They nodded and drove off.

How to respond to people who stopped to talk to me was one of the things that the Lord was teaching me. If this incident happened today, I would drop everything and go pray for the person. Those young men never called and I've wondered what happened to their grandmother many times. I did the wrong thing by not going with them right away.

> Teach me Your way, O Lord;
> I will walk in Your truth;
> Unite my heart to fear Your name. (Ps. 86:11)

I didn't get too far down the road before a small woman and her daughter, who looked about ten years old, stopped and encouraged me to help return prayer to schools. A little farther down another woman and her gray-haired mother stopped. They said prayer was needed in school. The mother gave me a five-dollar donation before they left.

As these people urged me on, I saw that prayer in school was very important to many people.

When I later entered a convenience store to get water, I met an Oklahoma City sheriff's deputy. An African-American about six feet two and 300 pounds without an ounce of fat on him, his sleeves were rolled up, revealing huge muscles. He told me that he was an ex-football player.

He sure looked like one, I thought.

"I'm tickled to death at what you're doing," the deputy said. "Carrying the cross will keep you in good shape anyway."

The two of us laughed about it.

"You are the man of the hour," the deputy said. "There would be a lot less crime if there was prayer in school."

I agreed with him. Since the Columbine tragedy, parents, teachers, administrators, legislatures, and law officers all over the country are arguing about how to stop crime in schools. The problem had already existed before Columbine; that incident showed us just how bad it was. Violence like that had already erupted in other parts of our everyday life.

After a few more words with the deputy, I headed out again and an Edmond policeman drove by, made a U-turn, waited for me in a little nook in the road, and gave me one of those "Are you crazy?" looks.

When I got near him, he asked without enthusiasm, "What's your destination?"

"Christian Faith Church."

He said nothing else, drove on, and passed several other times to keep an eye on me.

When I stopped to get water at another convenience store, I met a couple dressed in business suits, and their small boy. The lady approached me and said, "I own a little Christian nursery in Edmond. Do you carry the cross all over the country?"

"No," I told her. "This is my second trip. I have one more short trip planned." I had planned to carry the cross from Edmond down Broadway Extension to the State Capitol in Oklahoma City for my last trip.

When I said that, the woman started crying. Then she handed me a check.

I shook my head and told her, "I'm doing fine. Thank you very much, but I'm really okay."

She trembled as she pushed the check toward me. The look in her eyes told me to keep carrying the cross. She said, "Don't deny me."

I knew she was telling me not to stop her from obeying what God had told her to do. I took it and said, "God bless you," and went on my way.

The Lord, I believe, was teaching me how to handle gifts from people. I had always worked and paid my own way and been the person giving rather than receiving. I wasn't comfortable taking money from people, yet I had no authority to stop what God was doing in their lives. I decided then that if anybody offered me a donation, no matter what size, I would not decline it, unless I felt the Lord moving otherwise. By refusing someone's gift, I would be denying them God's blessing.

The check, I saw a short while later, was for $500. I wasn't out to obtain donations for my walk. Later, I gave Christian Faith Church a donation out of the lady's check and put some of it in the bank and left it there. I figured the Lord would tell me what to do with it.

The next day I became a member of that congregation. I had visited several churches over eight months and felt like this was the one the Lord had picked for me. The people were friendly, the choir was great, and I could really feel the presence of the Lord there.

But God had not picked my ten-mile walk to the State Capitol. I picked it myself. Two weeks after I walked to Edmond, the paper showed that another man had carried a cross down the same route I had planned. I thought it was God telling me, "I've got that covered. You're not going that route. You're finished."

I had no idea that I would ever carry the cross again.

Chapter Four
The Call to Carry the Cross to Columbine

I can do all things through Christ who strengthens me.
Philippians 4:13

One day six weeks later, as I worked at my cutting table, the Lord spoke to me again in my spirit.

"You are going to have a ministry called Bearing the Cross Ministry," He said. "You will give testimonies anywhere you can to draw attention to getting prayer back in school."

I thought me having a ministry was a cool idea. I was getting excited again, like when the Lord first told me to carry the cross. I was almost jumping up and down, I was so happy, but the Lord must have been letting that bit of news soak in before He finished.

Thirty seconds later, He broke the other news. He said, "Your first mission will be carrying the cross from Oklahoma City to Columbine High School in Littleton, Colorado."

Mentally, I quickly calculated the miles, thought of climbing the mountains into Denver, and my mouth dropped open. The whole idea was shocking. My insides froze up. All of a sudden I wasn't so sure I'd heard the Lord correctly. He was talking about me walking 700 miles! I thought, You've got to be kidding!

Stunned, I stared into space, multiplying the thirty-one mile walk to Purcell by twenty-five. *Oh, my God! That was impossible!* The radio was playing, and it was as though someone turned it up full volume. A person sang, "If the Lord said it, believe it. If the Lord said it, obey it."

I settled down then. The Lord, through the song, seemed to be reinforcing His message. I said aloud, "That's good enough for me, Lord God."

I immediately called my wife. "Lori, I need you to pray for me."

"Oh, no," she said. "What are you and the Lord planning now?"

Needing to be positive I had heard the Lord correctly, I said, "I can't tell you now, but please pray."

"Well . . . "

I needed her to stand behind me on each walk, but especially such a long one. If she did, it became our walks, meaning God's, Lori's, and mine.

"What do you want me to pray about?"

"The Lord is dealing with me about something."

"Something like what, Garlin?"

"Oh, just something. Will you pray?"

"Yes. I'll pray."

I knew I would obey the Lord and walk to Littleton, but it certainly seemed impossible. Had I really heard from Him? Had I imagined such a crazy idea? To be sure, I called Pastor Gadberry, who had received a vision from God before and who I thought would understand what I was going through.

"I believe I've got a new mission. I'm going to carry the cross to Littleton, Colorado," I said.

"If it came from the Lord," Gadberry said, "you know it. And if it came from the Lord, you need to obey it!"

That was practically the same thing the singer on the radio had said after the Lord spoke to me. I took Gadberry's words as confirmation. By myself, I knew it was next to impossible, but the Word said in Philippians 4:13:

> *I can do all things through Christ who strengthens me.*

It was summer then, and if I was going to do it before winter, we had about a month to get ready, and the first real step toward doing that was telling Lori. I knew the walk to Purcell had been hard on her and I wondered how challenged she would be by this one, but time was so short that I couldn't think about it for long.

A few days later Lori was in our living room sitting in a chair when I walked by her and said, "We're going to carry the cross to Colorado," and scurried toward the bedroom.

"What!" She shot to her feet and got on my heels. "No way. That's crazy!"

I didn't know what else to say.

"No way," she said and her eyes were a fiery green. "I do believe prayer needs to be back in school. I believe it can change some of the lives of high school students in a positive direction, but you're talking about walking 700 miles."

"I know."

"What about your knees?"

"I made it to Purcell on them."

"That's a little different than walking to Colorado," she said. "What about your hernias?"

"I'll make it."

"And lose the rest of your toenails?"

"I hope not. I've got better shoes now. I'm better prepared to walk this time."

"What about all your siding jobs?"

"I'll have to get them finished before we go."

Lori flopped into a chair in the corner of the bedroom. She didn't say another word, but I could tell she was still upset and didn't say any more. She was in as much shock as I was.

Right after I told her, I sang a few verses along with a song playing on the radio.

Overhearing me, Lori said, "My Lord, I hope God never calls you to sing because you'll never make it."

The humor broke the tension, and we laughed. But inside I

wondered about walking 700 miles to tell people that God wanted prayer back in school. In the end I decided that no matter how impossible it looked to me, God would use me to accomplish His will. It was my job to obey Him and the results would be His.

Before I picked out a date to start my walk to Columbine, I knew the only way I could walk that far before winter, honor my siding contracts, and get everything else done was to begin by walking weekends. Doing that would allow me to finish my siding jobs and condition me to walk full time. And I would also begin walking shortly after the Lord told me to.

While I sorted out those details, Lori struggled to believe in what I planned to do. "The pain I watched you endure walking to Purcell was fresh on my mind," she told me sometime later. "Why did God want you to walk 700 miles after the first walk had been so hard on you? The thought of going through 700 miles of that was unbearable! So I didn't mention it for a few days. I didn't want to discourage your faith, but I'm sure I did."

As I prepared to walk to Colorado, my stomach, which had been hurting for about six months, got worse. I sure didn't want to tell Lori.

"I don't know what's wrong with me," I told Carroll. "My insides are messed up."

"What do you mean?" he asked.

"When I put my hands on certain parts of my stomach, my whole inside hurts. I think it's serious. Please don't tell Lori because I don't want her worrying about it."

A month later my stomach started hurting even worse, and I started bleeding anally. One day after work, the pain forced me to go to the emergency room at the Veteran's Administration hospital. I called Lori from there and told her where I was and why.

"I can't believe God asked you to walk 700 miles to Colorado when you're so sick," she said. "I'm coming to the hospital."

"No. Just hold on a while. I'll let you know what's going on."

"I'll give you a couple of hours," she said after a few silent moments.

Veteran's ran several tests on me and discovered that my blood count was twenty percent lower than it was supposed to be. They wanted to hospitalize me for more tests and observation, but I had things going on and asked to be treated as an outpatient. Reluctantly, they agreed and set up an appointment for me to return for tests.

When I got home, Lori gave me some penicillin, an old prescription that I had around the house. It didn't stop the bleeding but did ease the pain. I did have an infection, the Veteran's had said, but I didn't think bleeding inside had anything to do with that. When I worked, I hurt so badly that I would almost cry. I got real tired and all I wanted to do was sleep.

Then something miraculous happened. During Sunday services at Christian Faith Church, Pastor Gadberry preached on healing. I thought the Lord had spoken to him about my condition, but I found out later that Lori had spoken to him.

At the end of the service when everybody stood for prayer before dismissal, the pastor asked if anybody needed to be healed. When he walked by with a bottle of anointing oil, I stuck my hand out in the aisle and he rubbed oil on the outside of it. Immediately my whole body heated up, it seemed to me to about 250 degrees.

I hung onto the back of the pew with both hands because I thought I was going to faint and fall over on the floor. I knew I was being healed.

Afterwards, I told Lori that I was healed and didn't need to go back to the VA, but she insisted that I go to the doctor to make sure. Of course not going back wouldn't have been wise.

If I was really healed, the doctor would know it. That's the safe way to respond.

I told Lori that my blood count was back to normal and that they wouldn't find a thing wrong with me. The VA performed numerous tests, and two weeks later called for me to come in for an examination of my upper gastric intestinal area. Lori, who answered the phone, got worried about that, but they told her they couldn't find anything wrong with me and that my blood count was better than it had ever been. I thought they only wanted to find something wrong with me.

I know the Lord healed me. I don't know if He did it so I could carry the cross to Columbine High School or not, but I sure thank Him for doing it.

I had asked Lori and Pastor Gadberry not to tell anybody about my walk to Columbine because I didn't want to get that crazy look from people again. At the same time I had to tell churches that God wanted prayer back in school. I had heard quite a few people talk about how much the country needed prayer in school, so I thought I could get some churches involved with the next walk. I personally visited preachers all over the greater Oklahoma City area. I got every kind of welcome there was, from "that look" to approval, but some of them stopped me in the middle of my pitch to tell me they weren't interested.

After that, I handed out flyers to preachers and pastors and secretaries at churches. A few churches were very interested, but I never got a response from any of them.

I then decided to start a petition to get prayer in school on the ballot in Oklahoma and visited a law library where I researched how to get that done.

A law librarian went out of her way to help me. She got me all the petition laws, but there were so many of them that I needed help. The librarian recommended a good Christian attorney who knew a lot about petition laws to help me sort them out. Through him I found out that the law had to be changed nationally.

The attorney said, "The best thing you can do is carry the cross to Columbine High School. It might draw some attention and encourage the country to vote on it."

I still needed to get the word out. So Lori and I made up press releases that explained when I would leave and showed my route and gave them to newspapers and radio and television stations so they might cover the event.

In the meantime, we shut down our business and paid everything for at least two months.

Lori and I developed a simple plan of walking. When I went alone, I would drive to the beginning point of that day's walk, park my pickup, and start out. I would tell Lori by phone when and where to pick me up. She would call me four or five times a day to check on me. We purchased two phones capable of reaching from Oklahoma City to Wichita so we could communicate over longer distances while I was walking.

When Lori went with me, she would take me to where I ended the day before and let me out. Then she would pick me up at the end of my walk. If I was in a dangerous area, she would stay close by to check on me.

Having learned that just any walking shoe wouldn't work for me, I purchased a pair of lightweight brand name canvas walking shoes. As soon as I put them on, I knew they were the right pair.

I also carried half a gallon of water, flyers to hand out, camera, tape player, radio, mobile phone, pen and paper, business cards, candy, and Ibuprofen. The total weight of everything I carried, including the cross, was about fifty pounds.

A few days before I left on the walk, I bought a canteen and a pouch for flyers I planned to give to anyone who stopped to talk with me. I also purchased a Bible for the Bernall family in

Littleton. One of the boys killing people at Columbine had asked their daughter, Cassie, if she believed in God. When she said she did, the boy shot her to death. The Bible was a gift I wanted the Bernall family to have.

We would return to Oklahoma City after each day of walking until we got so far away that we had to rent a room.

I had no idea how long it would take, but I wanted to get to Columbine before winter hit Colorado.

Our route would take us north on Interstate 35 through Wichita, where it turns into 135 north. At Salina, Kansas, we would take Interstate 70 west, which went all the way into Denver. I thought this route would gain the most attention about prayer in school from motorists.

That was the route we had figured out, but it wasn't the route the Lord had planned.

Chapter Five
"Let the Little Children Come to Me"

But Jesus called them to Him and said, "Let the little children come to Me, and do not forbid them; for of such is the kingdom of God."
Luke 18:16

I decided to leave for Columbine Saturday morning, August 20, 1999, and I invited anyone who had expressed an interest in the walk to meet in Edmond at Metro Church, located directly off Interstate 35, for a prayer service before I started out.

Fifteen people—more non–Christians than Christians—met at eight o'clock that morning. I was disappointed because there weren't more Christians, but the ones I loved were there.

The walk received very good publicity. A *Daily Oklahoman* reporter wrote a story. A reporter from the *Edmond Sun* was there, and after I began, a KTOK radio reporter interviewed me beside the interstate.

I had an adrenaline rush that day. But while I was excited about starting, I anticipated the hardest task of my life. Not knowing what was ahead and wondering how my body would hold up left questions in my mind. Once I started, I knew that I couldn't stop or turn back. God had picked me to do this and I felt responsible to see it through.

Lori remembered the first moments of the walk. "It was a pretty day to begin. I was excited. A week before we left, during prayer, God assured me that He would take care of you.

Suddenly all of my burdens and fears lifted, and from that moment I never worried about your health or safety on the walk to Columbine. I was at peace with it! I don't think I have ever seen you more at peace with yourself than that morning you left. I was very proud to be a part of it."

Finally, I headed out, fighting against the adrenaline to set a solid pace that I could keep up the whole day. Not far down the road, a truck parked a couple of blocks in front of me and a short heavyset man got out and walked back to me. Looking like a construction worker, he had tears in his eyes as he handed me a $20 bill and said, "The Lord told me to give you this donation."

He was crying so hard he couldn't talk and before I said anything, he got in his truck and drove off.

Although the donation wasn't large, the man's actions stirred up an understanding of the ways of the Lord in my mind. While the Lord had given me the task of carrying a cross, He had given this man the task of leaving an offering. Each of us was simply obeying God. Telling the country that God wanted prayer in school was a larger job than Lori and I or the fellow that stopped could do alone. None of us were important people. But God, in His unsearchable wisdom, drew people from all directions to accomplish a job. He could just as well have brought a man from China to leave me a donation.

It's sort of amazing when you think about it.

That day, I got to Guthrie, Oklahoma, fifteen miles north of Edmond, and we worked all the bugs out of how I would walk. I wasn't used to walking yet and I was a little tired at the end, but I had so much adrenaline pumping through me that I really didn't feel that bad.

That first day was not really a walking day but a day to gain media attention and it possessed all the anticipation and excitement that I could have hoped for.

Early the next morning, Sunday, I drove my pickup with the cross in it back to Guthrie, parked in town, and headed out.

Now in the midst of the big walk to Columbine, I couldn't shed a nagging concern. I had not heard anything more from the Lord since He had told me to walk to Colorado, and I felt a little insecure about what I was doing. I wanted to obey the Lord but I wanted to be reassured too. Since I hadn't heard anything from Him, I had a few doubts, and I was wondering why He hadn't said anything else.

When I had purchased the canteen, I had also purchased, for protection, a pocketknife with a three-inch blade from an Army surplus store. If anything happened to me, I wanted to be prepared.

After I had traveled about forty minutes, the knife, which was in the front pocket of my pants, got real hot. It burned my skin like an old Zippo lighter that was overfull of fluid. I pulled the pocketknife out, and looked at it, and the Lord spoke to me.

He said, "Throw it away."

Ignoring what I'd heard, I decided to put it in my back pocket.

Before I could put the knife away, the Lord told me again, "Throw it away."

Disobediently, I stuck the knife in my back pocket.

For the third time, the Lord spoke. He said, "Trust in Me one hundred percent."

I knew it was Him for sure then. His call for trust was enough assurance for me. I said, "Okay" and tossed it.

A mile later a Toyota pickup pulled up in front of me, and two guys in their early thirties got out. One of them was big and heavyset, and the other was average, about my size, but skinnier. The big one reached in the back of the truck.

I didn't know what he was going to get and thought, "Oh,

Lord." The Lord had just told me to trust Him and now I had the chance to do it, so I kept on walking.

The big fellow looked back at me and hollered, "We got you a cup of coffee here, man."

I felt a wave of relief. "Well, that's good."

The big guy talked with me about carrying the cross while the smaller man listened. When the big guy got back in the truck, the smaller man talked.

"I can't make it to church this Sunday because I'm working," he said. "I get a real blessing from seeing you carrying that cross. You are my contact with the Lord today."

Before I knew it, we were praying together and hugging each other and crying.

About to leave, the man said, "I'm sorry I don't have anything to give you."

"Man, you've given me more than anybody has," I said, my heart full of love for him and the Lord for bringing these men across my path. "God bless you."

He left crying and I left carrying the cross. All the aches and pains went out of my body. I was glad that I had trusted the Lord rather than a pocketknife. For the next mile or so I did nothing but cry and praise Him. I was humbled by how the Lord was using me. I was feeling good!

Since it was Sunday, I wanted to go to church if I could. At 10:30 I was midway between Guthrie and Stillwater, home of the Oklahoma State Cowboys. That's where I spotted a cream-colored church right off the service road, which I thought I could make by eleven, when Sunday services probably began. The church building had been a Stuckey's store some time ago. Walking faster now, at 10:59 I entered Vassar Church in Mulhall and service started a minute later. The sanctuary was neat with a small speaker's stand up front on a stage. I guessed there were fifty people in attendance.

Some of the congregation had seen me carrying the cross and

knew who I was from the newspapers. The pastor, whose name was Ralph Yost, according to the sign out front, turned to me and asked, "Will you say a few words?"

I remembered the Lord had told me I would give my testimony, but it still scared me. I sucked it up and walked to the front. I looked at the expectant faces, took a deep breath, and plunged into it. "I'm walking from Oklahoma City to Littleton, Colorado, to draw attention to the need for prayer in schools. I am also carrying a Bible to the family of Cassie Bernall."

A man in the congregation asked, "If there was prayer in school, would she and all the other students at Columbine be here today?"

I had heard that question before and replied, "I don't think anybody knows the answer to that. There's a possibility that two shooters may have listened and gotten to know the Lord. Allowing more freedom to pray in school doesn't mean the students will accept the Lord, but it means they will know they have a choice."

I had learned that, according to Scripture, forbidding children to pray was disobeying God.

> But Jesus called them to Him and said, "Let the little children come to Me, and do not forbid them; for of such is the kingdom of God." (Luke 18:16)

I expected someone to ask, "If we allow Christian prayer in school, won't we have to allow Moslems and Hindu and other religions to pray?" I was ready to answer it, but nobody did. I'm not afraid of letting the other religions pray. It's not like a boxing match between two equals: God is in one corner and His creation gone awry is in the other. Elijah showed in 1 Kings 18 that one man of God with God can overcome great odds. God just wants to get in the ring.

I concluded my testimony: "This is my second weekend of walking. I ask that you all pray for me as I make my way to Littleton."

I sat down and a little later a golden-haired woman wearing a white dress sang a song with the words, "there is no greater love than that of God for His children."

Her words seemed like they were coming straight from God: *God loves His children.*

When the service was over, Pastor Yost called me up to the front of the church, anointed me with oil, and prayed for me. I was near a front pew and I just about went out. I was so weak that if I hadn't held on tight to the pew I would have fallen flat on the floor. I sat down while the pastor ministered to others.

After he finished, another woman asked him if they could give me something and he agreed. It was humbling enough accepting an offering beside the road, but when these church people passed a plate for me, it made me feel like I was officially working for the Lord.

While the plate went around, one little boy walked over and gave me half a package of tic tac's. That really meant a lot to me because I knew it was all the little boy had. Giving me his tic tac's probably meant as much to him as someone else giving a $100 bill. He had given me one of his little treasures. I started crying.

Then a little girl about eight years old hugged me and said, "Thank you for carrying the cross and trying to get prayer back in school."

Her little arms were filled with love. I will always remember her thanking me for trying to get prayer in school. God knew how to pull at my heartstrings. I think that was His way of saying, "This little girl is whom you are walking for."

She made me think of my own granddaughter, Shelby, who was only one year old at the time. I wondered what school would be like when she attended? Would it be totally prayerless and totally godless? Or would Shelby be able to say that her grandfather and many others helped return the full freedom to pray to classrooms and not lose the right to honor God in school?

I thought about these issues most of the afternoon, long after I had left Vassar Church. The little girl had put a face on the issue of prayer in school. The idea of how much God loves our children and that He wants them to know Him hammered into my soul. God had emphasized this by telling me she was the reason I was walking. That whole event at Vassar Church, perhaps more than anything else, illustrated to me how vital prayer is. Now my heart was knit to God's heart concerning this cause.

I felt like I was fighting one of the biggest giants ever, this anti-prayer movement in our country, but I also felt like I had all the strength I needed.

Lori picked me up after I had walked sixteen miles. On the way home we stopped at a convenience store to get a copy of the *Edmond Sun* to see how much publicity had been given to the walk. I figured that if there was a story, it would be small. To my surprise the walk had about eighty percent of the front page and I purchased a stack of newspapers.

The next day, I talked with three preachers who were interested in my walk and gave them copies of the newspaper. Then I went to KTOK radio and asked if I could get on one of the talk shows. I also sent information to KNYD, a Christian radio station based in Tulsa and part of the OASIS Radio Network.

From this point on I thought the media attention would take care of itself, except for me sending press releases to media in bigger towns before I got to them. I felt that most of my legwork with the media was finished. All I had ahead of me was a long hard walk and I was anxious for the next weekend.

When I walked on the Sunday of Labor Day weekend, it was eighty-five degrees and overcast with the wind blowing at my back. I started out twenty miles from Kansas and planned to make it to the state line, where the turnpike begins. I couldn't walk on the turnpike, which began thirty miles south of Wichita, because it was against the law. I would walk to the toll road and return the next weekend to Wichita and start again on I-35.

Reaching the Kansas State line would mean I had made it through the first state and I would be able to see my progress and be encouraged.

From where I was walking I saw a pond with a bright yellow morning sun shining on it. Although it was early, we had a light blue sky with no clouds. The frogs were croaking and jumping and Black Angus cattle were standing beside the pond. Two trees with branches thick with rich green leaves shaded part of the pond. It was some of the beauty God put on this earth. When you're walking you get time to see things that are always there but you just never noticed.

I walked about twelve miles without anybody stopping. My attitude was a far cry from what it had been on my first walk when I expected nobody to stop. Now I looked forward to ministering to people and it was difficult for me to keep my spirits up when nobody stopped, and I felt like I was walking for no reason.

When I had already walked twenty-two miles, the state line was still another three miles away. I was tired and I didn't know if I could make it. I also faced a thirty-mile-per-hour head wind, and it was pretty hard going. The hot Oklahoma wind was taking a toll on my face, which was red from the sun and starting to blister. My lips were split and chapped. As I walked I moved the cross from one shoulder to the other because both were aching.

It seemed like the longer I carried the cross the heavier it got. Both knees and my feet ached. I was realizing how really hard a walk this was going to be.

Two miles from the Kansas line, I stopped at a roadside park and filled my canteen with water. I sat at a picnic table near a Hispanic family with four young children.

The man held up a sandwich and motioned for me to come

over. I supposed that none of them could speak English. I nodded and sat with them, one of the children on each side of me. Of course, we couldn't understand what each other said, but I was grateful for their kindness.

After they left, I laid down a short time, then took the cross to the Kansas line and called Lori to pick me up.

I had gone about twenty-five miles and was proud to have made it that far. It was the most I had walked in one day on the way to Littleton. I could feel that my body was getting built up. I could now walk ten miles before I felt it and could make twenty miles without much trouble. But now we were so far away from Oklahoma City that we had to drive to our starting point and stay the weekend.

I was eager for the next leg.

Chapter Six
Provision

The steps of a good man are
ordered by the LORD,
And He delights in his way.
Psalm 37:23

The next Saturday a Kansas highway patrolman pulled in front of me on the highway and my stomach tightened. I was south of Wichita and north of the toll road that began at the state line. The dark-haired patrolman looked a little upset, and I guessed he didn't like me walking on the interstate. While I watched him get out of his car, two younger patrolmen in another vehicle pulled into the median and spun around.

I thought they were going to turn the car over trying to get back to me. I don't guess one was enough.

The first patrolman approached me, his jaw tight. "Let me see your identification."

The other two got out and stood near their vehicle as I handed my driver's license to the officer. He returned to his car and called it in. I waited nervously. Their check on me didn't find anything, particularly a warrant. If they had found one, they would have had a reason to arrest me.

The first patrolman said, "You can't walk on the interstate. It's against Kansas law."

This was the first time I had faced direct opposition to my walk, and I didn't know quite how to deal with it.

I didn't argue with him. My very first thought was that I had done my best and the trip to Littleton was finished because the interstate was about 500 miles of my route. I didn't know what to do. Then it hit me that Satan was trying to stop me from carrying the cross to Columbine. And I thought that I had a lot bigger boss than the patrolman had. That got me pumped up. *God had said we were walking to Littleton and we would!* I was learning to put myself in God's mighty hands. I was one man walking beside the highway with a cross, and some people would say that was reason enough to lock me up. I knew I had to have enough faith to keep going.

> So Jesus said to them, "Because of your unbelief; for assuredly, I say to you, if you have faith as a mustard seed, you will say to this mountain, 'Move from here to there,' and it will move; and nothing will be impossible for you." (Matt. 17:20)

The young patrolman looked at the others, then, with a smirk on his face, eyed me again. He said, "Your trip will have to be postponed, boy."

I had been nervous and a little upset, but now I was mad. The patrolman had used "boy" as an insult.

I had tasted how African-Americans felt when they were offended this way. I didn't like it. In times past I would have argued with them and used a few choice words myself, but God gave me restraint. The first trooper hadn't shown me, an older man than he, any respect whatsoever. I'm sure the back of my neck had turned red.

I asked him, "Is it against the law to walk on the state highways?"

"No."

"My trip isn't postponed, then," I said and added a little more than I probably should have. "My trip's just been re-routed, boy."

The patrolman's smirk turned into a frown.

The tension was thick. I knew if I said any more I might be arrested. I held my breath.

"Okay, fella," the patrolman said, jaw still tight. "That cross is too big to get into the patrol car so you'll have to carry it back to the exit ramp."

I nodded and he drove off. I thought I had been very close to going to jail, and I had no idea what route to take or what problems another highway would present. I called Lori and told her what had happened.

"What are we going to do?" she asked.

"Meet me at the convenience store near the motel. We'll plan a new route."

Lori could tell how upset I was by the tone of my voice. "It's all right. We'll still walk. I'll meet you there."

I didn't like the idea of walking on Kansas state highways because they are a lot more dangerous due to narrow shoulders. The traffic wouldn't give me much room and my chances of getting hit would be higher. When I met Lori at the store, a Wichita police officer was there. I approached him to find out if the other policeman was lying. "Hello, officer," I began. "Do you—"

"It's against the law to walk along the interstate anywhere in the United States," he said before I could get my question out. The law officers had already discussed me among themselves.

But what he said wasn't true. I had checked and it was legal to walk on the interstate in Oklahoma. I hadn't thought to check out each state's laws, and now wished I had.

Too riled up to say any more, I walked away. In all my life I had never been treated so badly by the police, like a criminal. If they got on the criminals one-tenth as bad as they did me in Wichita there would be no crimes committed in the city.

It took Lori and I half an hour to decide on a route along State Highway 50 about three hundred miles west to Colorado. All I knew to do was go on. I wasn't quitting. I wasn't giving up.

The new route was more difficult and more dangerous than the interstate, but I was determined to make it. Satan could just back off. I was walking regardless.

We drove to Newton, Kansas, our new beginning point, about twenty miles north of Wichita to an intersection of Highway 50 and Interstate 35. Here, I started walking west with the traffic. A fairly new cement highway with deep green grass on the sides and in the median, it started off with four lanes and plenty of shoulder.

It was several feet wide and had warning grooves for four or five miles. The wheel on the back of the cross ching, ching, chinged all the way and made it difficult for me to hear cars coming up behind me. I hoped I didn't have 270 miles like that to go.

The police harassment continued to disturb me. They had done everything but frisk me. Was it really for walking illegally on a state highway or was it for carrying a cross? Did they plan to badger me until I gave up? Why would they want to do such a thing?

If the police treated somebody who worked for the Lord like they treated me, this country was in trouble. I already knew we were in bad shape as far as being a Christian country was concerned, but I had never dreamed that the police would make such an effort to stop somebody working for the Lord.

As I walked along, I worried that the police might see the "GOD WANTS PRAYER BACK IN SCHOOL" sign on the truck and arrest Lori. But she came by at about 10:30, when I was about ten miles out of Newton, and I felt a wave of relief.

Around eleven o'clock traffic got pretty heavy. A lot of people passed and honked and yelled out the window at me. I didn't know why the traffic had increased so much. Between Salina, Kansas, and Colorado I would have felt lucky to see anything alive on the roadside.

I realized that people had more time to read the sign because they were driving slower than they would on the interstate. I also saw a lot more beauty than I would have on the interstate. For an old country boy like me, there's nothing better than seeing the space and trees, the beautiful golden wheat, and feeling the wind in my face. All of God's work is out in the open spaces. The area showed that there's still a lot of beauty and a lot of good things left in this United States worth fighting for.

I concluded that the Lord knew what He was doing by having me walk down the state highway. I remembered Psalm 37:23:

> *The steps of a good man are*
> *ordered by the* LORD,
> *And He delights in his way.*

I think He means every bit of that verse.

An hour after I got started, the shoulder narrowed to only two feet wide in spots and traffic whizzed by me much closer than I liked. I had known that that would happen. Walking with the traffic presented a major problem. When cars drove in the lane next to me, I couldn't see them until after they had passed me. If I wasn't all the way over to the right, I had a chance of getting hit every time a car went by.

A few miles down the road, that very thing almost happened. A gust of wind struck my left side, blowing me to my right. Glancing over, I saw a thirty- or forty-foot blue mobile home trimmed in tan no more than six inches from me.

The thought flashed through my mind that "Newton was going to bite the dust in Newton, Kansas!"

With only a split second to react, I stepped over and grabbed the cross with my left hand to hold it down against my shoulder and keep it from hitting the motor home. If it had, it would have thrown the cross into me.

I froze as the mobile home roared pass. The gust from the tailwind slapped me. Shaking inside but still not moving, I watched the big blue chunk of rolling metal dwindle away.

After that, I thought working for the Lord sure made putting on siding for a living boring.

I walked about twenty-two miles before Lori picked me up and we drove to Hutchinson to find a room. The state fair was in town, which was the reason traffic was so heavy and also the reason that the cheapest room in town was about $100.

They kind of jumped the rates up with the fair in town. That's a whole lot of money to me, and I got a little bent out of shape because of it. So we drove back to Newton and found a room for close to $70. It was the cheapest we could find.

When I went in a convenience store the next morning, a policeman stopped me, asked for identification, ran a check on me, and went on his way. It was frustrating.

Lori let me out west of Newton where I had ended the previous day. It was rainy and very windy that morning, so I expected to be uncomfortable. And I didn't know what lay ahead of me with the highway patrol situation either.

This part of the state was flat and the wind rolled the golden wheat fields. There weren't many trees. The road ahead, however, had a good five-foot shoulder on a two-lane, cement highway. I had put on my red poncho and thought I would only make five miles before I'd have to quit due to the rain, but the weather cleared up by noon.

An hour after I got going, a trooper stopped me. I got a little upset but held my tongue. We went through that same check again.

An hour later a couple of state troopers pulled in behind me. My stomach tightened, and I thought, here we go again.

The driver, a stern looking man, got out. The other trooper remained in the car.

They ran another check on me, which was the third time that day. All the troopers on Highway 50 knew where I was going and who I was by then. I was getting used to being stopped and them running checks on me.

The big trooper asked, "Who are you and where are you going?"

"Garlin Newton," I said as Channel 3 News from Wichita drove by, spun around, and started back toward us. The patrolman looked at the news vehicle and back at me. I said, "I'm walking across Kansas on Highway 50 to Littleton, Colorado."

His attitude had changed. He smiled one of those smiles we all have seen, a you-know-I'm-smiling-but-I-really-don't-want-to smile.

I told him, "I'll try not to speed."

He handed my driver's license back, turned, and walked to his car as fast as he could. And he drove off before he got the results of his check. He couldn't seem to get out of there fast enough after the news people showed up.

The Channel 3 reporter, a dark-haired young man, had a microphone and recorder in his hand when he approached me. Another guy had a camera. The reporter asked," Where are you coming from and where are you going?"

"I'm walking from Oklahoma City to Littleton, Colorado."

"What would make you walk that far?"

"It was a vision that I received from God."

The reporter raised his eyebrows slightly. "Are you being sponsored by any church or religious group?"

"No, we are not. I really have not tried to get a financial sponsor."

"Do you think your walking will do any good?"

"I wouldn't be walking 700 miles if I didn't think it would do some good and if I didn't think it was from the Lord."

After a few more questions, the reporter handed me two tickets to the state fair. I knew I wouldn't use them because I didn't want to walk twenty miles, then walk around the fair in the same day. I took them anyway to give away.

I finished walking at close to four that afternoon because we had reached Hutchinson, twenty miles, which was our distance goal for the day. I expected to get back to Oklahoma City before dark.

Naturally, I was tired. We wanted to get home and wanted to watch the Channel 3 News interview of us, which didn't come on until 10 o'clock. I didn't want to stay in Hutchinson until then to watch it and drive back to Oklahoma City to go to work the next day. Lori wanted to see the newscast, however, and I saw her point. This might be the only time we would ever be on the news. We decided to stay and see it.

We walked around the fair until 5:30 before driving to Wellington, about twenty-four miles from Oklahoma, but we needed a television to watch the news. I told Lori that we could go to a motel for about two hours and watch it.

"A motel person would think we were meeting for a little hanky-panky," Lori said.

I hadn't thought of that and laughed, then replied, "If you find a good Christian person, I guarantee you they'll let us stay free and they'll say, 'Honey, whatever you want, we'll be at your service.' "

That didn't quell Lori's doubts, but we found a motel and I told the check-in lady that I was the person carrying the cross, and asked if I could rent a room for a couple of hours to watch the 10 o'clock newscast.

Very bubbly and outgoing, she said, "Honey, whatever you want, we're at your service. Go get that room. We'll do it for free."

These were the exact words I had told Lori, who was about as astounded at what she said as I was. The lady showed us to a room, brought us coffee and tried to buy a tape and record the show for us, but I insisted that we purchase our own tape.

While we were there, *Wellington Daily News* reporter Tracy McCue, wearing tennis shoes, arrived and interviewed me.

Then we went to Sonic Drive-In where the light was better, and he took several photographs of me and the cross.

I thought finding the room and the added publicity had made the day a success. But the Lord had not finished with His divine connections. When I put the cross in the pickup a few minutes later to head home, a man stopped by and gave me a $100 bill.

"The Lord wanted you to have this," he said. "You'll probably need it."

"Thank you," I said and I wanted to talk to him a little bit, but he was finished and walked on.

Later I thought about all that had happened that day and was amazed at how Christians worked for God and for other Christians. It amazed me how some Christians went out of their way to help me. By helping me they knew they were pleasing God. Christianity is a lot about helping another brother.

I probably learned more about Christians during my time carrying the cross to Columbine High School than the other forty-eight years of my life.

I am absolutely convinced that when God gives you a mission, you should do it. He may not give you a ministry such as Bearing the Cross Ministry, which he had told me to start, but as you move in obedience, you will grow closer to Christ and other Christians.

Chapter Seven
My Testimony

And they overcame him by the blood of the Lamb
and by the word of their testimony.
Revelation 12:11

L ori and I left Oklahoma City at about 4:30 the following
Saturday morning for Hutchinson and arrived at about
8:30. We had left then instead of Friday because our funds were
getting low, and with the fair still in town, the rooms would
cost $80-$100 a night. By leaving Saturday morning we only
had to pay for one night at a motel.

I knew the walk was getting hard on Lori and I was concerned about her. She was losing a lot of rest on weekends and
during the week she spent extra time keeping up with her reg-
ular chores and the things around the house that I could no
longer do. To compound the stress already on Lori, some family members told her to let me walk alone, which she ignored.

Not working Saturdays meant I put in longer hours during
the week to keep up with my siding jobs. I knew I couldn't
complete the walk without her. I prayed: "Dear God, give Lori
the strength she needs for this mission. Help her understand
the need for this walk and that this is our walk and not just
mine. Look after her and guide her. In Jesus' name, amen."

Although tired from the workweek, doing various jobs, and
the drive from Oklahoma City, I was excited about carrying

the cross again. When I started out, it was raining and chilly, with a temperature in the 40s, and my cheap poncho had a worse tear in it than I had thought. Water leaked in on me and I saw I'd soon be soaked. Wishing for something to keep the poncho from ripping apart, I found a pair of wire pliers and a piece of baling wire within a few feet of each other on the side of the road. I made a pin out of the wire and mended the tear. It was good enough to keep me dry. I couldn't have asked for anything better than that. I felt like God had provided for even that small need.

From the very beginning of the weekend, I had the feeling that I was going to get hit by a car or truck. I don't know why. It wasn't a message from God or anything. It was a gut feeling and I kept hoping everything would be okay. This was fear in my mind, perhaps prompted by a report I had seen on television about people getting killed beside the highway. In 1999, twenty-eight people had died that way in Oklahoma.

After I had walked a few miles, a man and his family in a white Chevy Blazer stopped to see if I needed a poncho. Although I had repaired mine, the wind had ripped it pretty badly and the man saw that. But the rain had quit by that time, and I told him no. A short time later another man stopped to see if I needed a place to stay that night, but I thanked him for being considerate and explained that we had a place already.

The rain started again and poured down until two or three, then a light mist fell on me the rest of the day. I could have used that poncho that guy offered me, but we made another twenty miles that day nevertheless. I got soaked and I was glad to see the day come to an end. It was cold, wet, miserable weather.

At eight o'clock the next morning, with a temperature of sixty-eight underneath a bright sun, I started out. My goal was Stafford, Kansas, about twenty-two miles away.

Before I left I saw Lori holding her hands out in front of her, her fingers straight, to keep from bumping them against anything. A skin allergy in her hands had bothered her for many years, and that morning her hands were so red and blistered that they looked like she had put them in a fire. They had hurt so that she hadn't slept that night and they were too painful to wash. In certain kinds of weather, especially, her hands became very painful. I had seen them splitting open with blood running out before. I had seen them chapped, peeling and itching. To get relief once before she had gone to a dermatologist, who split them open, applied an ointment, and put them under a heat lamp to help dry them out. She had lost all of her fingernails several times because of this condition.

Before leaving on the walk, she had filled a prescription for them, but since the medication usually helped her for only ten days, she was holding on to it until she really had to use it.

I wanted the Lord to heal her. As I walked, I prayed, "Lord, sometimes I feel like I ask too much from You, but Lord, it's my wife's hands I pray that You will heal before we get finished with this mission. In Jesus' name, amen."

I was walking beneath a light blue, cloudless sky. Open plains on one side of me reminded me of the rolling landscape in parts of Oklahoma. As far as I could see, the dark gray two-lane highway with a narrow two-foot shoulder lay in front of me. Off the road in an open meadow of green and brown grass about eighteen inches tall, several buffalo gawked at me. They are some mean looking hombres with those huge, shaggy black heads. I took a picture of them.

Shortly after that, a well-dressed guy stopped and gave me a few words of encouragement about prayer in school and a $10 donation. I thought he was a priest because I saw rosary beads and a cross laying in his seat. Later, a Kansas State trooper going in the opposite direction honked and waved. Then a heavyset guy and his young son stopped by, talked, and gave me a few dollars to buy lunch.

I walked out of Reno County and into Stafford County, about twelve miles from my destination, the city of Stafford. Many people who drove by waved or honked.

Because we had made pretty good time that day, I thought we would get done early and get back to Oklahoma City at a decent time. But Pastor David Ford, an outgoing man with light-brown hair, and his wife Rebecca, a tall oriental lady, from St. John Baptist Church stopped by and asked if we would give a testimony at their church that night. We agreed, of course.

All we had to wear were blue jeans and tee shirts, so we had to give our testimony in them.

After I finished walking, we cleaned up at a truck stop, drove to the church, and parked in their lot an hour before the service. Pastor Ford saw us when we drove up and told us he had invited the local paper, the *St. John News*, and the Methodist church, among others, to hear my testimony.

I got that scary feeling in my stomach. The crowd he had invited was getting bigger and bigger by the moment, it seemed. I think he told everybody in town.

I felt like I was under the gun, but I would do my best. I reminded myself that carrying the cross to Columbine was a great gift from God. And Him letting me speak on His behalf before His people was a privilege too. I started praying that the Lord would give me the strength to do it.

The *St. John News* reporter, Pam Martin, interviewed me before the church service began.

Afterward Lori told me, "I was in the lobby a while ago and these people are expecting a great testimony from you."

That brought the butterflies back. I told myself jokingly that they thought this great speechmaker had come to town to give a testimony to end all testimonies. Carrying the cross was one thing, but this was totally different—and terrifying!

I remembered Exodus 4:12 and depended on it.

"Now go; I will help you speak and will teach you what to say." (NIV)

Before I knew it, time had flown by, and church had started. As Pastor Ford placed a wireless microphone on me, I said, "I haven't spoken much like this."

"I'll give you some good advice."

I expected him to tell me how to shake off the butterflies. "What is it?"

"If you go to the restroom, make sure you have the microphone turned off."

I couldn't help but laugh, and that settled me down a little.

When I got up to speak, not only were quite a few people there and the local newspaper, but they also had two cameras on me. Nervously, I reviewed everything we had gone through thus far. When I finished, a silvery-headed woman asked, "Does Cassie Bernall's family know you are carrying the cross to Columbine High School?"

"No."

"Do they know you're bringing them a Bible?"

"I plan to leave the Bible at their church rather than give it to them personally."

A neatly dressed woman in her mid-fifties stood up. "I have a granddaughter who attends a different school than Columbine in Littleton. She told me recently that people there are aware of you carrying the cross to Columbine."

That was good. People were hearing about the walk and the need for prayer in public school. After I finished my testimony, Pastor Ford and Rebecca asked us to stay so they could take us to dinner, but we had to drive back to Oklahoma City that night. They asked for a rain check.

My legs and back ached and my shoulders were tired, but I was holding up pretty well. I had worn quarter-size blisters on my right foot, one on the heel, dime-size ones on the other foot, and one behind one little toe. I had walked twenty-three miles that day. I was still far enough away from Littleton to imagine the hard grind ahead, but I had built to a kind of rhythm and I felt more positive than ever that I would make it.

We got home at one o'clock in the morning, and I got up six hours later to go to work. I was tired when I got to bed and tired when I got up.

Nobody said it was going to be easy to be a Christian.

Chapter Eight
Perseverance

You therefore must endure hardship as a good soldier of Jesus Christ.
2 Timothy 2:3

The next Friday Satan attacked me, I felt sure, to stop my walk to Columbine.

I had had the flu all week, complete with nausea and fever, and expected to have a rough walk. Besides that, Lori didn't go with me.

When I got to a rest stop on I-35 just before the Kansas State line, it was raining. I planned to sleep in the truck rather than a motel for several hours to save a little money before driving to Stafford, Kansas. I had left home with only $43, and that was donated.

My not working Saturdays had cut our income and our money was getting kind of slack.

From where I stopped to sleep, Lori could still reach me on the cell phone, but when I got into Kansas, I would be on my own. I knew I had to trust the Lord to take care of me that weekend.

It quit raining before I took off, but the wind was blowing and I was cold. The sky was gray and the area was flat with a lot of green trees. The road was two lanes and blacktopped.

I walked out of Stafford at about 7:30. I was uneasy being out there without Lori. I really had never felt unsure of walking, but I left my pickup in Stafford and I didn't know how I was going to get back to it. The next town, a little place called Macksville, was twenty-two miles away. And when I got there, there was no assurance that even a store would be open. I didn't know if it had a motel, so I didn't know whether I would have to sleep on the side of the road or what.

I was loaded down with toiletries, about ten pounds more than I normally carried. I had taken food with me, particularly beef jerky to eat on the way, since I wouldn't pass any place to eat lunch.

I had only gone a couple of miles when the stomach virus came on me again, and I got so sick I could hardly walk. I had stomach cramps, diarrhea, and fever. I felt like I was next to death. My joints hurt with each step and I had no strength whatsoever. Being out there with diarrhea was no fun.

I was paying that physical price to accomplish what God had told me to do again, but the illness wasn't too large to overcome.

When I realized I had gone fourteen miles, I was determined to get to Macksville.

Nobody had stopped all morning long and that disappointed me. It was as though I was out there all by myself, but I kept thinking that God was with me.

Five miles from Macksville I felt so sick I had to lie down under a tree. I thought I would feel better after a little rest and make the last few miles.

A woman in a new maroon Chevrolet pickup stopped while I was there. Still some yards away, she poked her head out the window and asked me, "Do you want something to eat?"

"No, ma'am," I told her, "I'm doing fine." I didn't want anything to eat; neither did I want her to get close enough to catch that virus from me.

I rested another ten minutes before I started on, hoping the diarrhea didn't hit me again. Another round of that was all I needed.

I had gone about twenty-one miles when the blister on my foot started bothering me. Every time I put my right foot down, it hurt, and I limped from the pain. By now it was 4:30. Ahead, I could see a water tower, a grain silo, and a white house near Macksville. I couldn't tell if it had a gas station. If it did, I would find someone in a pickup to give me a ride back to Stafford.

A little later, I saw the sign: Macksville City Limits. I could see a small, white wood frame church with a small steeple, several houses, and a service station. There was a windmill with a water well pump on it on one side of the road and a graveyard on the other side. I was so sick that I felt like I needed to be in that graveyard right then.

I hid the cross behind a church, where I would return for it when I got my pickup. I got a drink of water and waited outside the station to hitch a ride to Stafford. An hour passed before anyone stopped, so I filled my canteens and headed back to Stafford after walking twenty-two miles already with the flu.

In a mile only five cars passed me.

Things didn't look good.

In an hour and a half, it would be dark. Still feverish, my legs, particularly my joints, continued aching.

Finally, a guy in an older blue pickup with a loud muffler and tailpipe stopped just before dark. He was wearing farm overalls. He said, "It's hard to get a ride around these parts."

I nodded. "I found that out. Thanks for stopping."

The gentleman let me off in Stafford.

I had walked close to thirty-two miles that day and I was exhausted. After I got my truck, I drove back to Macksville and got the cross, then drove home. It had been a long hard day. I didn't walk the next day because I was too sick and sore.

Walking to Columbine was getting harder because of driving

back and forth to Oklahoma City each weekend. It was taking a toll on me in several ways. I got little work done on Friday nights because I had to get up early Saturday mornings to get back to where I had finished walking and the drive back to Oklahoma City on Sundays after walking, all day added to my fatigue. Work on Mondays was torture because I was so tired.

Yet I was making real headway in miles, and the people along the way who had stopped so far had acknowledged the need to return prayer to the schools.

Chapter Nine
Difficult Steps

If I take the wings of the morning,
And dwell in the uttermost parts of the sea,
Even there Your hand shall lead me,
And Your right hand shall hold me.

Psalm 139:9–10

I started out from Macksville the next weekend more than 400 miles from Columbine. That first day I walked about twenty miles through the towns of Bellefont and Spearville before stopping. When I took off the next morning, it was misty with the wind blowing. I went twenty-two miles to a hill at the edge Dodge City, where I saw a large feed lot packed with cattle of assorted colors.

From here I could see down into the city. When I reached a point in view of the sign that says, "Dodge City. Visit Boot Hill Downtown," a man in a little black truck pulled over in front of me and got out. In his early thirties, he had dark brown hair to his shoulders and wore a black, waist-length leather jacket. He was a real hippy type, I thought, although I knew better than to judge a book by its cover.

The fellow was smiling big as he walked toward me. "When I topped the hill and saw you carrying the cross," the man said before I got to him, "I said what a blessing! This is great!"

I had learned that some people stopped not because of prayer in school but because they had seen the cross and needed to be ministered to. "Hello."

"This is great! This is great!"

I shook his hand.

"This is great!" he said again and began walking alongside me.

"I've had some problems," the man said, "and I didn't know who to talk to about them. You're it."

I didn't feel an ache in my body right then. Somehow when I ministered to people, I was able to focus on them rather than my own physical pains.

"I am a recovered drug addict," he said. "Because of Jesus"— his eyes lit up—"I've been clean ten years."

"That's great news."

"I'm looking for the right woman to marry. I have a son and need a wife who will help me raise him in a God-filled home. I haven't found her yet."

"Let God pick her out for you," I advised him. "He'll help you. Just wait on God."

He walked with me about a mile, the first person to walk with me on the trip to Columbine. We finished talking and I watched him head back to his pickup.

He really blessed me. He made the whole weekend worth the walk.

Friday evenings and early Saturday mornings were usually difficult for me to get motivated to walk because of the fatigue. Somehow every Sunday before I ended the trip, God would make it all worthwhile. He would give me a blessing like this guy.

I noticed I was almost in the famous cow town where Kansas State Highway 50 splits. One route goes through downtown and the other one around the outskirts of town. I chose to go downtown, even though it was longer, because more people would see the sign. Heading into town, I saw a group of bikers who were wearing a lot of black leather with patches of skull and crossbones and daggers. They were riding Harley Davidsons, carried chains, and wore tee-shirts. They rode by and looked at me funny. I stuck my arm straight up in the air, pointing toward heaven.

Getting to Dodge City meant Lori and I had accomplished our aim for that weekend. I was proud of that. I was sure to get to Garden City, about halfway to Littleton, by the next weekend and I planned to walk full time after that.

We were close enough to start counting down the days, but our money was getting shorter too. Although we had paid our bills two months ahead, I had to find a way to finance the rest of the walk, which was going to take three weeks to finish. I had failed to sell three horses, and with less money coming in from my business and hardly any money in savings, I wondered how we would afford the motel rooms.

We returned to Kansas the following Friday night and I walked twenty-five miles that Saturday. Then we drove to Garden City to check out the highway shoulders and the ten miles immediately west of town. I didn't want to cheat on this journey, but we decided to start walking about twenty miles east of Garden City because the shoulders were too narrow for the first ten miles for me to walk without getting hit by a car. There was really no room to walk.

The next morning I left around 7:30. It was sixty-five degrees, and I had gotten a good night's sleep and felt rested. The weather was perfect; the sun was shining. I took off in an area of rolling hills, which meant I wouldn't see cars near me until they got fairly close. The prairie grass was thick beside the asphalt highways. Here and there I saw long lines of cedar trees, which had been planted to keep new crop seed from blowing away before it started growing.

After walking about nine miles, the shoulder narrowed to six inches and the terrain changed. The area became sharply hilly and the roads curvy. Just beside me, off the road, was a twelve-foot ditch. At that time, I was walking with the traffic,

my back to cars driving by. Because this was much too dangerous, I switched to the other side of the road, which had about a
one-foot shoulder, and faced the traffic. Although it was safer,
I still couldn't see cars coming toward me because of the hills
and curves. With the wind blowing most of the time and the
wheel on the back of the cross keeping up a steady clink-te-
clink-te-clink, I couldn't hear the cars either.

One foot *was* wider than six inches but not room enough for
a car and me. When a car came into view, I had to get off the
highway into the ditch. If I didn't see or hear it soon enough, I
had to jump off immediately. As well, drivers weren't getting to
read the sign because I was facing them.

One foot was still pretty narrow, so I walked about twelve
miles partially in the highway.

Lori went ahead of me to each mile intersection keeping an
eye on me all the way because it was so dangerous. She didn't
feel very good that weekend either. She had that old flu that I
had had the last two weeks.

Finally past that treacherous area, I walked on the grass next
to the road, but it had rained a lot in the early part of the weekend and when the grass played out, I was in solid, black clay
mud. It was hard to take a step. The mud overlapped my shoes,
and when I pulled one foot up, it made a sucking sound. When
I put the other one down it sunk into the mud. I practically
drug the cross over this stretch. It was a rough haul.

My canvas shoes, while made for walking on sidewalks or
level ground, didn't provide me the side support I needed on
a surface of grass and mud where I walked most of that day. I
only walked on the shoulder a tenth of the time.

As I trudged through the mud, I saw a patrol car coming
toward me and cinched up inside. I hoped the trooper didn't
stop because I was having a hard enough time as it was and
didn't want to be hassled again. I was not walking on the highway, for which the trooper could have stopped me. When he

drove on by, I was relieved. I had been right, I thought, he couldn't have done anything to me.

But then the patrol car turned around in the middle of the road and came back.

Correction. The patrol car passed me, then stopped, pulled off beside the road behind me, lay back on the side of the road, and watched me walk for a little while. I wondered what was going on, but kept dogging along. Finally he started the car and went on without saying anything to me.

That was curious. I guess he just wanted to see what I was doing.

A big man and his wife stopped while I was on a dangerous curvy stretch of road, told me to keep going, and gave me $50. That really helped us out and it perked me up a bit. I thanked them and I got back up on the shoulder where it was more than a foot wide for some distance, still facing the traffic.

Suddenly a car roared behind me. It sounded like it was on top of me and a chill went up my spine. Practically every hair on me stood on end. A little dark blue sports car sped down the lane I was in. As I jumped to one side, the car zoomed past.

It came within five inches of me and around another car. That was the closest call I had had since I started the trip.

Shaking inside, I kept walking. That had been too close. I had to shake the fear off and pull myself together. "Lord, protect me," I prayed. "Thank you, for not letting that car hit me."

Between Dodge City and Garden City, about fifty miles, packing houses lined up one after another. Long, rusted, red steel pipe fenced in the lots where they fattened cattle to butcher. Each lot was about a half-mile long. Large white metal feed barns sat in the center of the lots. The cows were packed almost too tightly to fall down and trucks kept up a steady growl of traffic, hauling in live beef and shipping out butchered meat. Thousands of cows fed in those yards.

And it smelled like it. Passing by the feedlots with the wind blowing in my face was pretty disgusting. The mixture of the waste of tens of thousands of cows was worse than standing in a sewer. The smell, like some angry beast, leaned on me for miles.

Finally, several miles past those lots, I saw a wide shoulder. Walking in the grass and in the lumpy mud while I carried the cross had about worn me out.

After eighteen miles, I could see Garden City about three miles away. It was flat land with a trailer park on one side of the road and a convenience store on the other. It was about 4:30 in the afternoon. Knowing that I had gotten out of a place where there was no shoulder and seeing Garden City was refreshing. And the next stretch had a shoulder.

I had seen a lot of things beside the road, some I looked closer at, but most I passed by without a second thought. As I neared Garden City, I saw a white envelope lying in the ditch. It was no big deal, I had seen a bunch of them, but something told me to pick it up. That something told me that it had money in it. I walked past, trying to ignore the impulse, but the prompting to pick it up was so strong that I went back and got it.

Inside the envelope was a check for almost $900. The amount startled me. I did a double take to make sure it wasn't one of those fake checks you get in the mail sometimes. It was real. I figured the people it belonged to were either sick to their stomachs already or would be as soon as they noticed it was missing. Their names were plainly written on it.

The funny thing was that it came from the same town in which we gave the testimony, St. John, some 150 miles back. I thought that was an interesting coincidence. Was this one of those examples of giving and receiving that the Bible speaks of, I wondered? People in St. John had honored and blessed me. Now I had a chance to honor and bless someone from St. John.

I put the check in my bag and later mailed it to the owners.

As I entered Garden City, I saw Lori waiting on me. It had been a hard day and she could probably tell that by looking at me. I was thrilled about reaching my destination but too tired to celebrate. She met me and carried the cross for the last block and a half.

I had walked twenty-five miles that day. I don't know how, except through the Lord's strength. All told I had gone more than 300 miles.

We had come so far that we couldn't really drive back and forth on the weekends any longer. When I returned to Garden City, an important milestone on my walk to Columbine High School, I would walk full time.

Chapter Ten
Taking up the Cross Daily

Then He said to them all, "If anyone desires to come after Me, let him deny himself, and take up his cross daily, and follow Me."
Luke 9:23

Twenty days later, October 31, Lori and I returned to Garden City to complete the walk. During those twenty days, I caught up on all my siding work and purchased an old travel trailer (on a credit card) that we fixed up to sleep in. The trailer, I thought, would reduce our living costs. My plan was to park it somewhere for three to four days at a time, then move it on to the next destination. By walking every day, I had figured out, it should take fifteen days to carry the cross 300 plus miles to Columbine High School.

When we got to Garden City Tuesday morning, we tried for several hours to find campgrounds to park the trailer, but the cost was $20 more than we had budgeted. We were stretched financially as it was, so we decided to look for a cheaper place to park it. Then we saw its tires were bad. They looked new, but I guess they had sat too long and rotted out. We had no choice but to purchase four new ones.

Offsetting that expense somewhat, the First Assembly of God Church in Garden City allowed us to stay in their parking lot three days for free. It was inconvenient trying to find a place to park the trailer, I saw, and wished I hadn't gotten it.

After we got the trailer set up, I called a guy at a talk radio station in Garden City to see if I could get on his show. He wasn't interested but asked in a disc jockey's voice, "Are you doing this for the money?"

The question made me mad. *What money was he talking about?* The timing for the question was bad too, especially after we had charged $1,000 for the trailer on our credit card and spent $400 on tires for it.

"I'm not doing it for the money" is all I said.

Later that day I visited the *Garden City Telegram* and told them what time I would start walking the next morning in case they wanted to do a story on me. I went from there to Channel 11 and gave a red-haired young woman the same information.

Starting at 7:30 that morning, I walked through downtown Garden City. The wind was blowing at about twenty miles an hour and it was chilly, about thirty degrees. I was wearing gloves, but my hands were still like ice. However, the weather forecast called for sixty-five that day and seventies all week.

The *Garden City Telegram* reporter, Heidi Tomsen, and the Channel 11 TV station people found me walking that morning at about the same time and shot pictures.

After we finished I walked through Deerfield. A man had asked me to walk by the school so his children and others could see me. I knew I couldn't walk on the school grounds, but I didn't want to disappoint those young ones. When I got there, I stayed on the sidewalk to keep off their property. As I approached the school, a one-story tan brick building with windows all along one side, children poked their heads out the windows and waved at me. They reminded me of that little girl at Vassar Church, and I felt that determination rise up in me again. Yes, Lord, I thought, I'll finish this walk for them.

A very small town, many of Deerfield's citizens offered me dinner and the school officials were friendly.

I made it to Lakin that evening, a walk of twenty-two miles. My goal for the next day was Syracuse, about twenty-five miles.

The *Garden City Telegram*, which came out in the afternoon, had made my walk front-page news. As I took to the road that next morning, many people waved and honked and gave me the thumbs-up.

I guess they read the newspaper. Each response energized me.

After I left Lakin, the shoulder narrowed to eight inches, little space for me, and angled down forty degrees into a ditch about ten feet deep. Moving along the top part of the ditch, my left foot was on the decline and my right foot on the grass.

Walking on that kind of angle put a real strain on my hips. And it was tearing up my feet. Every time I put my left foot down it rubbed on the side of my shoe. I could feel new blisters forming on my feet and the ones I already had growing worse. Every step was an effort. One foot hit long and the other hit short. And I had to drag the cross several miles because the back kept sliding downhill.

Other problems plagued me on this stretch. Cockle burrs stuck to my socks and little rocks got inside my shoes, forcing me to stop frequently to clear the burrs and shake the rocks out.

It was rough. I guess that was why I hadn't walked that far by noon and I was exhausted. I was hurting so that I didn't know if I would hold up. I saw what I was made of on that stretch. I prayed for strength a lot that day.

By the time I had walked ten miles without a shoulder, the friction had rubbed more blisters on my feet. I also could carry the cross only on my right shoulder because I couldn't switch it to the other side like I usually did. If I tried to carry it on my left shoulder, it slid straight downhill. It rubbed me pretty bad and burned my shoulder.

Ahead I saw at least two more miles with no shoulder. The sight took all the air out of me.

As worn out as I was, five deer in a field of deep green maze caught my eye. A beautiful dark tan, they had their white tails stuck in the air and were trotting around. I stopped for a few moments and watched them, admiring God's beauty for a few seconds. Then they hopped away from my line of sight and disappeared in the maze field.

After I had walked thirteen miles that way, I got up on the highway and hoped cars would move out of my way. I couldn't walk in the ditch any more because of the pain. I felt like I was playing Russian roulette, and the cars were the bullets.

For a mile more I walked on the edge of the white line. Then I heard an engine roaring and got that cold chill in my stomach. A white-haired man driving a big yellow sedan rushed at me from behind. It was one of those Russian bullets I feared so much.

I could barely see his head over the steering wheel, and he was barreling right for me, about to take me out.

I dove for the ditch and the sedan roared past. I landed on my feet and managed to hang on to the cross. It seemed every muscle in my body trembled. The sedan sped on, swerving from one lane to the other with blue smoke gushing out of the tailpipe.

I guess he didn't see me. My heart was beating so hard that I thought it was going to explode.

It took me a couple of miles to gather myself. After almost being hit, I looked behind me every time I saw or heard a car. When one was headed toward me and another came from the other direction, I jumped back on the shoulder. If only one car headed my way, I could remain on the road and the vehicle would swerve around me.

An older man with a white beard and partially gray hair, accompanied by his stocky son-in-law, stopped and talked with me a good while. They wore overalls like farmers and looked like they had been working in a field. They said I wouldn't find a shoulder until I got to Syracuse, fourteen miles away. Then there were good shoulders, they said, all the way to Colorado. They also explained that from the Colorado State line to Lamar, about forty miles, there was no shoulder, but the road from Lamar on had good ones. I thanked them for their information and went on.

At the Hamilton County line the time changed from Central Standard to Mountain Standard. I hoped that meant I got to walk an extra hour. Here, there was little traffic or houses, so I felt like I was in the middle of nowhere. I did see an older cemetery with a red rock, knee-high retaining wall around it. It was about an acre in size with a lot of headstones.

From about eight miles away at the top of a hill, I could see the small, tightly clustered city of Syracuse. I made out four grain towers spread about the city. About half a mile from me, I saw an old house set just off the highway and walked over to see if I could get water. By this time I had drained my canteen because of the hard walk. After I knocked, a lady came to the door. She was very friendly, although a little leery of me. I don't blame her, living out in the middle of nowhere, and here's some guy walking along carrying a cross. I got a drink of water and she let me fill my canteen.

She said, "There's been a lot of people come by my house, but there's not been anybody carrying a cross before."

I wasn't a bit surprised.

She gave me two apples and they really hit the spot. She reminded me of the woman in Mark 12:42 who gave the two mites, which were worth a fraction of a cent. Those two apples might have been all she had.

I walked twenty-three miles that day. The terrain was the hardest I had ever walked. I don't know how I made it that far, except the Lord helped me. If I had walked twelve miles that day, I would have considered myself very lucky.

Lori picked me up five miles from Syracuse.

The next day we got up early and moved the travel trailer to the place of the two men who looked like farmers. They had given us permission to leave the trailer on their property for a few days.

We were very grateful, because they didn't look like well off people.

It seemed like I had blisters on eighty percent of my feet. One of the farmers had seen me limping and given Lori a grayish colored salve that they used on irritated cow udders for my feet.

With the wisp of a smile on her face, Lori eyed the salve, then me, and asked, "Will you use it?"

"At this point I'll use anything," I said.

The hernia belt, which had two straps that fit around each of my legs, had rubbed raw places that bled off and on. The braces had also worn spots just above and below my knees. My shoulders and back were slightly stiff but gave me little trouble. My feet were giving me the most trouble although I had rubbed some of the udder cream on them that morning before I left.

I was less than fifteen miles from the Colorado line. I walked through Syracuse on five-foot shoulders, which was easy compared with the previous day. I never would have thought a thing like that could have made me so happy.

"Praise the Lord for nice shoulders to walk on," I said loudly.

In town, I laid the cross down, went inside the *Syracuse News*, and stepped up to a long counter. A young lady who had long brown hair and was on the other side of the room met me and asked, "May I help you?"

"Would you like to interview the man carrying the cross?"

Her brown eyes perked up. "Oh, yes! Do you know when he will come through town?"

"It just so happens that I do know," I said, unable to resist stringing her along.

She smiled broadly. "When?"

"Now." I gave her a big grin that she didn't seem to understand. "I'm the man."

She looked at the *Garden City Telegram* on the counter, saw my photograph on the front page, and her face brightened. "Where is your cross?"

"Outside."

She hopped to a desk, grabbed a camera, went outside, and took a few pictures of the cross and me.

"When do you plan to get to Littleton?"

"On November 20 I will be forty-nine. If I could make it to Littleton on that day it would be one of the best birthdays that I could ever have."

"Do you think this will get prayer back in school?"

"Not really, but I hope it draws attention to the problem of the lack of prayer in school and maybe it will contribute to getting prayer back in school."

"Are you making the trip by yourself?"

"No, my wife Lori is with me."

"How many miles can you walk a day?"

"About twenty."

She pointed at the *Garden City Telegram* article. "This is about the neatest thing I have ever read in my life."

Her enthusiasm excited me and after the interview I got back on the road with vigor.

Lori caught up to me four or five miles out of Syracuse, parked the pickup beside the road, and walked back to me. She was crying.

"What's the matter?" I asked.

"I met a man who read about you in the *Garden City Telegram* this morning. He has been looking for you. He said he was very much in favor of getting prayer back in schools, but something about his eyes told me that his health wasn't good."

"Did he tell you what was wrong with him?"

"He found out this week that he has bone marrow cancer. He wants you to pray for him about that."

"What's his name?"

"Bob Petrus."

"Is he saved?"

She nodded. "He's right with God, but he owns the Syracuse Motel and other stuff and is worried about leaving too much of a burden on his wife."

"We'll go back and talk to him when I finish today."

Still crying, Lori got back in the truck and left for Syracuse.

I kept on walking but I was thinking about the man who wanted to talk with me about his disease. We were barely making it each day, but ministering to people like that man was what living for Jesus was all about. The Lord would take care of us, I was sure.

I could see that God meant to bless people from many different backgrounds through Bearing the Cross Ministry.

A couple of miles farther, a Kansas State trooper, a sandy haired man in a pickup passing me on the other side of the road, slowed, rolled down his window, and hollered, "Praise the Lord."

"Praise the Lord," I yelled back and went on. I got a better response from the troopers when I left Kansas than when I entered. I didn't know if the trooper said "praise the Lord" because I was carrying the cross or because I was only nine miles from the Colorado border and would soon be out of his state. At least they were treating me friendlier.

I had almost reached Coolidge. From there Colorado was two miles away. My heels were so sore that I almost tiptoed when I walked, so the udder salve hadn't helped much. I knew I had to do something about my feet before I could go on.

Lori was waiting for me in town with a sandwich and orange juice. She looked awful good to me, and so did the sandwich and juice.

When I got seated, I took off my shoes and socks. The blisters on the back of my feet had puffed up about a half inch and were aching badly. They were water blisters of some kind and filled with blood. I grabbed a knife.

Loretta was frowning at my feet, the knife, and me. "That looks awful, Garlin. What are you going to do?"

"I'll have to relieve the pressure so I can finish today," I said. I cut along the blisters, which released the blood. Then I dried my feet and put on a different pair of shoes and clean socks. I didn't have any wrappings for my feet. I still had two miles to go to the state line, but I was determined to make it regardless of how badly my feet were hurting.

For the next half-hour I walked as much on the balls of my feet as I could. Finally, ahead, I saw Lori waiting for me. I gave her the cross and she carried it into Colorado.

One sign read, "Leaving Kansas." The other read, "Welcome to Colorful Colorado." I said, "Praise the Lord."

I finished around four o'clock, having walked sixteen miles. The blisters had slowed me. We put the cross in the truck and returned to the Syracuse Inn to see Bob Petrus.

I had never prayed for a person with cancer before, and I asked God to give me the words I would need.

We walked into the motel lobby and I saw a gray haired man with a hint of worry in his face sitting in a chair. Standing near him was a petite red-haired woman about his age. She was dressed in a pretty green dress. I grinned at the man and he grinned back.

He pushed himself up, but it was a struggle. He looked weak as he extended his hand. "I'm Bob Petrus. This is my wife Beverly."

"I'm glad to meet you," I said to each of them as I shook their hand.

Bob said, "I talked with your wife earlier today and I want to thank your wife and you for coming over."

"We're glad to do it."

Bob talked about his motel, which was very nice, a large

motor home he owned, and a caboose that he had restored. Then he said, "These things don't mean a thing! After I found out I had cancer and may not be here much longer, I realized that the only thing really important is God and how you spend your life. When people tell me to have a good day, I think that every day that God gives me is a great day."

Beverly was about to cry and left the room.

These were sobering words that hit home with me. I had come to minister to Bob that evening, but instead Bob was ministering to me. "You're absolutely right," I told him. "I guess most of us tend to forget that."

I grabbed both of his hands and prayed silently that God would heal him.

Lori joined us, and gently taking Bob by the hand, they went outside. I was glad she did because God has given her a soft heart for people.

I saw Bob breaking down and crying. I think that was something Bob needed to do.

L ori said later what she and Bob talked about after they walked outside.

Bob told her, "God has given me strength through prayer and I have been at peace ever since I accepted God into my life."

"Praise the Lord," she replied. "He is wonderful."

"I've fallen in love with Him."

Lori then prayed for Bob. "Dear God, please heal Bob and comfort his wife and family. I know You love him and I know he loves You. Tell the doctors what to do for Bob and make the medicine work in his body."

A s I watched Lori with Bob, the Lord brought to my mind 1 Corinthians 1:3:

Grace to you and peace from God our Father and the Lord Jesus Christ.

I felt like everything would be all right with Bob and his family.

I saw Lori hugging Bob and patting him on the back and they came back inside.

Bob didn't look as worried now, but peaceful. "I will go to the hospital a lot in the next few weeks," he said. "My brother is being tested to see if he could be a bone marrow donor."

"I pray that he can," I said. The problems I had with my feet and knees didn't seem like much of a problem after listening to Bob.

He said, "You two will always be a part of my family."

Although we had just met Bob and Beverly, I felt as though we were related, too, and I thought Lori felt the same way.

Bob offered to let us stay in his motel or trailer park for free, but we already had a place.

Lori and I called it a day and headed for the trailer.

Chapter Eleven
Colorado

" 'A servant is not greater than his master.' If they persecuted Me,
they will also persecute you."
John 15:20

I started out the next morning inside Colorado, beneath blue skies and a golden yellow sunrise with a temperature in the fifties. I planned to get as close to Lamar, Colorado, as I could, and it was thirty-two miles away. This particular stretch ascended slightly, but it wasn't a hard climb and it led into a pretty area. Trees were plentiful and the brown grass extended out of my sight. About a half-mile south of me were railroad tracks. The road was elevated and I could see a valley below me on each side. While on my right three white-tail deer grazed, on my left ten or twelve hunters wearing orange and red vests over army camouflage fatigues were walking in a line. They had dogs and rifles.

By the time I made it to a little town of about 900 people with the pretty name of Holly, the first city on Highway 50 inside Colorado, Lori had gone ahead to do laundry. Four feet of shoulder paralleled the two-lane highway out of Holly. The road was hilly and wound through wheat fields, and railroad tracks crossed the highway and dwindled until they looked like one long metal line.

A city policeman drove by, did a double-take, then came by again a little later but didn't stop. Shortly after that, Lori and I, with the cross in the back of the pickup, went inside a convenience store in Holly for lunch. While we were there, a couple of policemen entered and sat in the booth behind us.

One policeman, sounding deeply puzzled, said, "I've lost the guy with the cross."

I almost spit out a mouth full of juice. Since the town was not that big, I wondered how they could have lost me. I looked at Lori and started to laugh a little, but she elbowed me in the side to make me stop. She was holding back laughing herself.

Then the other policeman said, "He's right behind you."

Lori and I grinned at each other.

After lunch I walked to within four miles of Lamar before we went back, got the travel trailer, and parked it at a campground west of town. The next day would be Sunday and I planned to walk to the trailer, which was about twelve miles, and stop for the day to give my feet a rest.

I had developed a daily regimen to keep my feet as well doctored as I could. At night I poured alcohol on them to keep them from getting infected. The next morning I would put a liquid coating on the blisters with a fingernail polish-like brush and let it dry. It left a thick skin-like layer. Then I placed cloth pads over the blisters, powdered my feet and toes, and put on two pair of socks.

At this point of the walk, it took fifteen minutes to doctor my feet. I didn't complain.

I now rejoice in my sufferings for you, and fill up in my flesh what is lacking in the afflictions of Christ, for the sake of His body, which is the church. (Col. 1:24)

I started out at about nine o'clock the next morning four miles east of Lamar on a shoulder three feet wide and near an open field of thick prairie grass that was almost completely brown. While the sky was a rich light blue, the temperature was in the sixties and the wind was blowing. It was a nice day for walking.

It took me about an hour to get to Lamar, where I would leave Highway 50 west and take Highway 287 north. Lori was waiting for me in a Wal-Mart parking lot. As I neared her, three slender, young Hispanic men in baggy blue jeans a few sizes too big and plaid shirts headed toward me, pointing threateningly.

I couldn't hear if they were swearing or not. They crossed the street from the Wal-Mart parking lot about one hundred feet from me and kept coming toward me.

About that time a police car drove by. I had been hassled enough by police already; now I was glad to see them. I don't know if the officer knew what was going on, but he slowed to about five miles an hour and kept eyeing those guys. When those young men saw the police watching them, they all turned and headed in different directions.

Whatever they were up to was no good.

I had put my trust in God and wasn't worried, but it may have been different if I had gotten face to face with them. I was glad the police drove by.

I had four more blocks to reach downtown Lamar. As I waited for a green light, a low rider with music blaring so loudly that it shook the ground drove up. The windows were tinted too dark for me to see who was inside. But the car stopped next to me, the music lowered, and a window rolled down. A dark haired man in a white tee shirt and blue jeans stared out.

He smirked as he leaned across his seat. "You crazy old freak carrying a cross!" Then he cursed, seeming to call me every name he could think of.

I stared back; we were eye to eye for a few long moments. I wanted to tell him what I thought, too, but forced myself to bite my tongue. Had I responded, he may have jumped out of the car and attacked me. So I just stood there. Perhaps I was too shocked and surprised by what he said to answer.

Thinking about what happened later, I didn't know why I

wasn't expecting this kind of treatment, since Jesus said it would happen.

> " 'A servant is not greater than his master.' If they persecuted Me, they will also persecute you." (John 15:20)

Knowing that Jesus had said it and had suffered didn't make me feel any better at the time. The man's words were like wounds, but I still didn't respond.

When the light changed, he drove off.

> The LORD is my light and my salvation;
> Whom shall I fear?
> The LORD is the strength of my life;
> Of whom shall I be afraid? (Ps. 27:1)

I don't know what type of vocabulary he used when he spoke to other people, but I hope it wasn't the one he used on me. I was glad to see him go on, because after the shock wore off, I was getting a little mad myself. I knew some people didn't like what I was doing, but I thought they would have toldl me in a different way.

A block and a half later, the scene with the guy still playing in my mind, three teenagers in a Chevy slowed down beside me and gestured obscenely. They were hollering and cursing and laughing like idiots, and I was shocked. Within eight blocks I had gotten more negative responses than the rest of the walk put together.

These incidents happened so quickly that I was beginning to get a little paranoid, but I had to let it go. I recalled verses in Psalms and Ephesians that helped.

> Yea, though I walk though the valley of the shadow of death,
> I will fear no evil;
> For You are with me;
> Your rod and Your staff, they comfort me. (Ps. 23:4)

Therefore take up the whole armor of God, that you may be able to withstand in the evil day, and having done all, to stand. (Eph. 6:13)

I wondered why they were treating me so badly. Then God revealed to me that they weren't hollering at me but at the cross and what it stood for. I realized then that the youngsters hadn't had time to read the sign. They started acting up when they saw the cross.

This was a real sad part of the walk for me. These people had no respect at all for the God of the universe.

I carried the cross out of town, but a few miles outside the city another teenager drove by and cursed me.

Most of the ones hollering, gesturing, and laughing at me in Lamar were sixteen to eighteen years old. They acted like Jesus Christ was nothing.

A lot of good people lived in Lamar, but more people there pointed and laughed and hollered bad things at us than elsewhere. It made me feel like I had leprosy. They acted like they didn't want me there. They thought they were giving me the finger, but I was representing Christ, so it was Him they were giving the finger.

While the people in most towns encouraged us, tried to give us food, and offered us space for the trailer, in Lamar we experienced the reverse. It gave me a funny feeling. Maybe the Lord wanted me to take this walk to find out how some people hated Him. What a sad country this would be without God.

If those teenagers had prayer in school, would they have acted differently? Maybe. Would they have known that there was a God and given the Lord the respect of being their Savior? Maybe. But at least allowing prayer in school would have given them the chance to act differently and honor Him. We all know that while we had prayer in school, Native-Americans were mistreated, African-Americans were denied rights and even hung, and women were treated as inferiors. We weren't perfect.

However, we honored God and tried and continue to try to correct some of the evil things we've done to our own people. Sometime the old ways are better.

I stopped walking about three that afternoon. It had been a different kind of day. I had almost lost it with those kids in Lamar. I didn't know if it was my temper or wrong thinking or what. I was very disappointed by the way I had been ridiculed. It left a bad taste in my mouth.

I've heard Christians say rejoice at persecution, but few of us in this country have really experienced it. It's much easier to say rejoice than it is to do, especially for a person as young in Christ as I was at the time. The ugly words and gestures were real, like the spit that hit Jesus was real, and they were meant to wound me. Mentally that was the hardest day of the walk.

Lamar isn't a bad town; Lori and I made a lot of friends there. If you look around any town, you will see the kind of teens that we had problems with. But afterwards I was depressed and had to draw strength from the Lord.

> *When you pass through the water,*
> *I will be with you;*
> *And through the rivers, they shall not overflow you.*
> *When you walk through the fire, you shall not be burned,*
> *Nor shall the flame scorch you.* (Isa. 43:2)

That night I prayed for those children and for our country.

Before I started out the next day, Monday, November 8, I left a press release at a radio station and went to the *Lamar Daily News* where I met John Kennon, a large man with thinning brown hair, who took notes for an article and pictures of me carrying the cross.

"I'll catch up with you tomorrow while you're walking and take more pictures," Kennon said.

I told him about the cursing and gestures and asked, "John,

will you not put all the bad things that happened in the paper? This is not why I'm walking. I'm doing it for our children."

Kennon nodded. "I'll do the story about the positive things about your walk."

At another Lamar radio station, KVAY 105.7, I did a long interview about the basics of the walk.

It was nine o'clock before I started out. The weather was great, fifty-five degrees with a light chill in the air. The weatherman mentioned the unusually mild temperatures for November. I thought it was a blessing from God.

I wanted to get as close to Eads as possible, but it was thirty miles away. Highway 287 here had four lanes with six-foot shoulders and a ten-foot wide grass median.

A red-haired Colorado trooper stopped and told me that I could walk on the highway if I faced the traffic. Looking out for my welfare, he smiled and acted professionally. I appreciated him stopping and treating me like a human being.

I generally walked with the traffic, if the road had a good shoulder, so motorists could see the sign. It was safer the trooper's way, facing the traffic, and I would obey the law.

As I walked, I listened to KVAY 105.7 at 11 o'clock that morning. I bet eighty percent of the news was my interview. After the newscast the radio people talked a little more about me carrying the cross.

One DJ said, "The way Garlin is walking he should make it by his birthday on November 20."

Then the other one said, "Good luck, Garlin!"

After the ridicule of the previous day, open encouragement lifted me.

No sooner had the show finished than people in passing cars started honking and waving. Several people stopped and told me that they wanted prayer back in public schools.

Down the road, I saw two police cars waiting ahead of me, and thinking they were waiting on me, I tightened up inside. But a few moments later a hearse and a long line of cars pulled into the road. They were a courtesy escort for a funeral. I was relieved.

I was about to enter Wiley, where I could see a school and three blocks of houses. Men were working on an unfinished Conoco station, so I couldn't get water or snacks. Since Eads was about twenty-eight miles away, too far for me to make that day, I had to stop at one of the houses along the way to refill my canteens. Kennon from the *Lamar Daily News* hadn't yet shown up to take pictures, so I was concerned that he had changed his mind about writing an article for the paper.

North of Wiley there was nothing but open fields and brown grass about a foot high. The houses were a mile or more apart. When I walked by one small, white frame house with wood siding, a woman yelled out at me. "Would you like to have lunch with us?"

I could see her husband beside her.

Wearing a long gray dress, she stepped out the door. The screen slammed loudly behind her. "Will you?"

It was 12:30 and I was pretty hungry. "I'm looking for a reporter from the *Lamar Daily News* to interview me and take some pictures," I said. "If I get off the highway, he'll miss me. If it weren't for that, I'd have lunch with you. I'll stop by tonight after the walk and visit with you."

"That will be great!" she said cheerily. "I heard the report on the radio about what you were doing and our family is behind you. Have a safe trip and God bless you!"

I kept going and ran out of water near Kiowa County. It had been about six hours since my last drink and it was eighty-five degrees. My mouth and throat were dry from a fifteen-mile-an-hour wind blowing in my face. My tongue felt like sawdust, but there was no place in sight to get water for miles in front of me.

Half an hour later a yellow 1979 Ford sedan badly in need of a paint job, and with a lot of rust around the fenders, slowed down in front of me. The Ford's brakes squeaked as it stopped.

A Hispanic man, who was in his late forties and hadn't shaved in a few days, got out and walked toward me. I had worked on harvest when I was young and recognized dust on him that would have come from harvesting crops. This was the time of the year the harvest would have ended.

Then he started crying, grabbed and hugged me and kept on hugging me.

"I saw you carrying the cross and I had to stop," he said. "You're spreading the good news of the Lord."

He couldn't speak English very well, but people had told me that I didn't speak good English either, so this man and I communicated just fine. I told him, "Thank you for stopping. I appreciate it."

"I'm going back to my family in Mexico," he said. "I work in the United States. I'm taking them money."

He had come from the north and couldn't see the sign. I explained where I was going and why.

"Praise the Lord," he said, started crying again and started hugging me again. "I'm going to tell my family about seeing you carry the cross. Follow me." He led me to the back of his car, lifted up the trunk, and pulled out a glass gallon jar of water with newspaper wrapped around it. He took the lid off and handed it to me.

I took a long gulp. It was hot, but I thought it tasted better than any water I had ever had.

While I drank, he pulled an arm full of fruit from the front. Banana peelings and an apple core were in his trash sack on the front seat. It looked to me like fruit was all he was eating on his way back to Mexico.

He handed me a large sack of apples and oranges and a bunch of about twenty bananas. He tried to give it all to me, but I set all of the fruit on the hood of his car.

"I don't need all of it," I said. I took two oranges and a couple of bananas from him.

He hugged me some more and started crying again, then got in his car and headed toward Mexico.

He had shared what he had, just like we read about in Matthew 25:35:

> *For I was hungry and you gave Me food; I was thirsty and you gave Me drink; I was a stranger and you took Me in.*

After the man left, I was filled full of joy. I prayed and thanked God for sending him and the blessings of food and drink and fellowship.

Kennon caught up to me then, took pictures, and interviewed me further. I knew we would make the *Lamar Daily News*. Most of the news people I had spoken to had run stories, so I felt the publicity was going well.

Kennon said I had gone about twenty miles that day. So I thought I had done pretty well. Actually, when I calculated it myself, I had walked about twenty-four miles.

I had started out the walk to Columbine averaging sixteen miles a day, and by this time I averaged twenty to twenty-five miles daily. But for the next few days I had to suspend the walk because of a doctor's appointment in Oklahoma City on November 10. We went back on the ninth, so I didn't walk that day, the tenth or the eleventh. That gave me three days for my feet to heal. When we returned, we would be about 175 miles from Littleton. I was in striking distance of the finish line.

Chapter Twelve
"Remember Me, My God, for Good"

Remember me, my God, for good, according to all that I have done for this people.
Nehemiah 5:19

While back in Oklahoma City, Lori and I caught up my father's affairs, I rescheduled my VA appointment, and we enjoyed sleeping in our own bed. I doctored my feet and wore sandals most of the time. I visited longtime friends at Balkan Siding who knew about the walk.

The owner, Elaine Balkan, who has light brown hair and was dressed in a dark blue business suit, asked me, "How far have you gotten?"

I use to work for Balkan, and every time I saw Elaine after I started walking to Littleton she would ask me what kind of progress I had made. "Over five hundred miles."

"I hope you're going to tell me about some of the people you've met on the way."

"I will. I'm 175 miles from Littleton. We'll leave in the morning to finish the walk."

"You're going to do it, aren't you?"

"Oh, yeah."

She and the other owners gave me a check for $200 for the walk. I was surprised and Lori and I really needed it. God had supplied our needs again, as Matthew 6:8 says:

*For your Farther knows the things you have need of before
you ask Him.*

I left there to get a haircut. The African-American shine man
at the barbershop greeted me with a big smile. "Can I shine
your shoes for you?"

I looked at my feet. "I've just got on old tennis shoes."

"I can paint them for you," he said with a hint of excitement.
"No charge."

I remembered that a woman had once washed Jesus' feet and
dried them with her hair. I felt a little like a stand-in for Jesus
because I really didn't know this man well, but he wanted to
give what he did for a living for the cause of prayer. I climbed
into the chair. "Okay. Thanks for offering."

"Your barber told me that you are walking to Littleton,
Colorado, with a cross," the shine man said. "This is my way
of contributing to the walk."

"When I get finished, I'll bring you some newspaper clip-
pings on it."

The man nodded. "I'm looking forward to it."

On Friday, November 12, Lori and I returned to Colorado
through the Oklahoma Panhandle. There, we stopped in
Guymon to give the *Guymon Daily Herald* an article. While the
paper in Woodward didn't interview me for a story, the
Woodward radio station did. Back at Lamar we found that the
Lamar Daily News had run a huge story. Then the Associated
Press picked up the story and it went nationwide.

All this coverage occurred while we were in Oklahoma City.

The *Denver Post* had informed the *Lamar Daily News* that they
wanted to follow me all the way into Denver as a story. That
morning's *Denver Post* already carried an article about the walk.

Lori and I were overwhelmed with all the publicity carrying
the cross had received. I had not dreamed that the story would
go out like it did. Getting covered by the Associated Press was

something we had hoped for, but it was almost unbelievable when it came true.

At about eight o'clock in the morning on November 13, I started out for Eads, Colorado, four miles away. The weather was a little nippy. A fifteen-mile-an-hour north wind cooled the fifty-four degree temperature. The sky was blue with rolling clouds, the land was flat, and the road looked like new pavement with cement shoulders. It was like walking on a sidewalk.

I felt refreshed after the three days rest, which had been good for my blistered feet.

Soon I walked into Eads, which had an elevation of 4,213 feet, more than 3,000 feet higher than Oklahoma City. The locals told me that it got harder to breathe the higher up you go and that it takes a toll on you. I was concerned about it, but the mere walking uphill itself put an extra strain on my body.

While in Eads, I tried to call the *Denver Post* reporter but didn't get him. Then I ordered a hamburger in a fast foot restaurant. After I had paid for my meal, the owner, a sandy haired man, brought out my hamburger *and* my money. He said, "Your money's not any good in my business."

I figured he had seen me carrying the cross down the road. "Thank you."

"You're welcome."

"Do you have a newspaper in Eads?" I asked.

"Yes, but I don't think the guy who owns it will put you in his newspaper."

"I've got to try anyway," I told him. After I finished eating, I went to the *Eads Lasierra* newspaper. I asked the man there if he wanted to do a story on me.

A guy with dark brown hair in casual tan pants, he gave me a peculiar, but not unkind, expression. "You've got enough coverage. Everybody knows who you are. It wouldn't do any good to cover you."

There was no need for me to linger there and I got on the highway again. I was 165 miles from Denver and twelve miles from the town of Wild Horse. Past midday now, the temperature had climbed to seventy degrees. I walked five more miles before a stocky, red-haired Colorado highway patrolwoman pulled up in front of me and slowed down. I cinched up inside again, suspecting she wanted to run a check on me. I was wrong.

After getting out of the car, she walked back to me. She was smiling. "Your daughter, Ammie, wants you to call her."

My relief that she wasn't going to hassle me quickly changed to concern at my daughter's sudden request for me to call.

I must have shown it on my face because the trooper quickly added, "It was not an emergency."

I was relieved again. Ammie and her husband Randy Timms, a race car driver as well as a dispatcher for an Oklahoma City trucking line, had kept tabs on my whereabouts via truck drivers along the highway. The trooper gave me an 800 number for Ammie before leaving. I would call her at the next town.

By 4:30 P.M. I had walked twenty miles into Cheyenne County. At 4:44 the sun had already gone down. In the twenty minutes before darkness fell, I walked almost another two miles and found a place to wait for Lori to pick me up. Later that evening I called Ammie and updated her on my progress toward Littleton.

The next morning, because the truck didn't want to start, I left late out of Lamar. Finally, at ten o'clock, I was headed for Kit Carson. My route took me to Wild Horse, then Aroya and Hugo. Limon was seventy-one miles away and Denver 148 miles.

It was about sixty-four degrees and the wind was still. As the people driving by honked and gave me the thumbs-up, I thought about what happened way back in Lamar. Maybe four or five people there had cursed me and gestured obscenely. It had only taken that many negative people to give me a bad attitude regardless of all the people who gave me good signs and support. I realized that I had been dwelling too much on the bad. Perhaps that's something too many of us Christians do. In my case Jesus warned me that I would be persecuted, so I should have been prepared to handle it.

At Kit Carson I drank iced tea and filled both of my canteens, which I did when I could because the distances between houses were so long. I didn't want to get too thirsty with such a long walk ahead of me. Twelve miles later in Wild Horse, I had emptied one container and didn't see a store to refill it. I did see two churches and two houses. My only choice was to get water at one of the houses. The first one, right on the main highway, was a tan-colored mobile home trimmed in dark brown. I saw an antique washing machine, an old two-man crosscut saw, and antique pots and pans. The place looked like a flea market. I spotted a water faucet sticking out of the side of the house and knocked at the door. It opened and an elderly lady peered out.

She looked a little mixed up, I thought, before I asked, "Can I get water and fill my canteen?"

Frowning, she said, "I don't know a thing about it."

There was something wrong about the way she looked at me. "You got a faucet out here. Can I get a drink of water and fill my jugs up there?"

"I don't run the faucet. I don't know a thing about a faucet."

"Well, okay. I guess I'll see you then." Afraid that I might be scaring her, I headed to the other house a mile out of town, but also right on the highway.

It was a blue frame building with a white roof. I knocked on the door several times, but nobody answered. I then looked around for a water faucet. When I saw a privy a hundred yards behind the house, I realized I wouldn't find water there.

I had to meet my mileage quota with the canteen I had left. While I walked twenty miles that day, seventy-five percent of the traffic was semi's and none stopped.

The next morning, Lori and I ordered breakfast at the Trading Post Restaurant, where the owner had tried to buy my lunch the previous day. A waitress told us, "The guy that owns this place wants to buy you breakfast, if you won't get offended."

I said, "We're a cheap date this morning. We'll take him up on it."

The free breakfast really helped us out financially, and that same morning a young couple gave us $20, exactly enough money to fill up the truck.

I began at about ten o'clock, late again, because we moved the trailer. It was another beautiful day with a few large cotton white clouds surrounded by a blue sky with a touch of light gray in it. The temperature was about sixty degrees and I had five-foot shoulders to walk on. I stepped briskly because I started late and wanted to make twenty miles by dark.

Lincoln County was an open plain that climbed gradually and reminded me of the Oklahoma Panhandle, with more elevation. At the top of hills, I could see for miles in front and behind me. There were no trees, just an ocean of light brown grass dancing as the wind blew through it.

I was climbing into the mountains, which were growing sharper. It was getting harder to walk because I would get to the bottom of a mountain and head back up; then do it all over again.

On Monday, the next morning, we moved the trailer to Hugo, where a guy who owned a motel let us stay for free. Lori talked to a policeman in Kit Carson to see if I could walk on Interstate 70 into Littleton. The officer wasn't sure and called somebody else who said he knew I was on my way to Littleton.

This man said, "If he puts a foot on our interstate, we're going to put him in a police car and escort him to the state line."

I told Lori, "Most definitely we won't be going the interstate."

Going up and down the hills all that day, I made nineteen miles. That evening, when I finished, I was close to Limon. My route would take me through Limon on Highway 287, which was also I-70, then to Highway 86 and sixty miles into Franktown. From Franktown I would walk north on Highway 83 and turn west on Highway 88, which is Arapahoe Road in Littleton.

So far Lori and I could not have asked for better weather. In the next five days there was one chance of rain. And the temperature hadn't sunk below forty.

I had really held up better than I had thought I would. I had learned to walk without bending my knees very much to keep the arthritis from hurting in my joints. Lori said I looked like I had lost ten pounds. By this time the skin on my face was kind of leathery and cracked from the heat and wind and had a few scabs on it. My ears had a few scabs on them too. My fingers were split open and I had to tape them up. It could have been worse. It could have been cold and my ears and feet could have been frostbitten.

I had gotten tired every day I walked, but most days I really looked forward to it. I hoped the Lord would be just a little bit proud of me for my obedience. I recalled how Nehemiah wanted his God to think of him.

Remember me, my God, for good, according to all that I have done for this people. (Neh. 5:19)

Remember me, O my God, concerning this, and do not wipe out my good deeds that I have done for the house of my God, and for its services! (Neh. 13:14)

I was so close to finishing that I began wondering what I would do when the walk was over. I knew after I accepted the Lord that my life would never be the same, and I knew my life would never be the same after the walk. I felt compelled to serve the Lord in some capacity, but I didn't think it would be carrying a cross again, other than from Oklahoma City to El Reno. That was a thirty-mile trek and was not very far anymore for an old stepper like me. There was more to Christianity than attending church, so I wouldn't only go to church every Sunday.

If you're a Christian and you really believe in Him, you must work for Him. I had learned not be surprised at what the Lord tells you to do. It's doing what you never thought you could that makes living for Christ so exciting.

When I entered Hugo, 5,046 feet up, I had already made twelve miles that morning. I saw a welding shop and a cross atop a steeple on a little Baptist church with white wood siding. It was fit for a Norman Rockwell painting. Four blocks down, I saw the travel trailer, where I would stop for lunch.

A police officer stood outside his car with one hand on the door and a phone in the other as he called in. His leg was cocked up on the running board of his car. He watched every step I took, and he made sure I saw him calling in.

After lunch, I was a couple of miles out of Hugo, when a thirty-five foot long cream motor home trimmed in burgundy with custom burgundy strips pulled up beside me. I stopped at the door and waited to see who would get out. When the door opened, my grandson Colby, a brown-haired four-year-old, was standing there. What a pretty sight he made! The youngster bounded down and I dropped to my knees to hug him.

My oldest daughter Windie and son-in-law, David, stepped out behind Colby. They traveled all over the United States setting up displays for Wal-Mart.

Windie gave me a hug and said, "Hello, Dad."

"Hello," I said and took a soda from David. I asked them about where they had come from and where they were headed and showed them my feet. As they talked, I put my shoes back on. In my head I could see Columbine not many miles away. I had to get going. I wanted to finish this thing.

Windie must have sensed my anticipation and asked. "When will you make it to Columbine?"

"I really don't know, but I'm beginning to get excited about finishing the trip," I told her as I stood. "I better get going."

"Let us know when you get within a day or so," she said.

"I will," I said, and they left after a few more minutes.

Farther down the road, I put my sandals on to give me relief from the blisters on the back of my feet, but they weren't walking shoes and I didn't wear them long.

Watching the sun go down and darkness fall, I saw Lori ahead in the truck at the mile marker. I was all but finished for the day. Then a '92, badly dented, maroon Dodge minivan with dark tinted windows drove slowly by me then turned around.

I was excited at the chance to finish the day ministering to somebody.

The van pulled in front of me onto the shoulder and waited there. I thought that was odd because most people who had stopped normally got out. As I neared the passenger side, the window rolled down and I saw two Hispanic men, a driver in his early thirties and another older man. I leaned my head almost in the passenger's window. I smelled beer and saw beer cans in the seat. The driver, who had glassy eyes and was extremely fidgety, had a beer can between his legs.

I had a bad feeling about then, pulled back, and motioned for Lori to bring the truck down. At the same time, I kept my eyes on the two men.

"Why are you carrying that cross?" the younger man asked roughly.

Realizing that this could be trouble, I didn't answer.

"Why are you carrying that cross!" he screamed.

The passenger told the driver, "It's okay, man."

The driver barked, "Answer my question!"

Moving back, I was glad I was on the passenger side of the van. "I'm carrying the cross for the Lord."

"Carrying that cross is ridiculous!"

Lori drove the truck beside me. I told the man, "I'll see you."

The driver kept staring at me.

I backed away, keeping my eyes on him. I was concerned that he might have a gun or something and quickly loaded the cross in the truck, which was running, and got in.

As Lori pulled out, she asked, "Why did you stick your head in that car?"

"I thought the man had something to tell me."

"Did he?"

"No, Lori. They're trouble."

As we drove off, the guy in the van watched us leave.

I was very glad to get away from those two. The Lord had watched over us.

> *The God of my strength, in whom I trust;*
> *My shield and the horn of my salvation,*
> *My stronghold and my refuge;*
> *My Savior, You save me from violence.* (2 Sam. 22:3)

After walking twenty-six miles that day, we were three miles from Limon and one hundred miles from Columbine. And it was only Monday. I realized we could make it to Littleton by Saturday, or even Friday.

I could see myself striding into Littleton.

Chapter Thirteen
Into the Mountains

Pray without ceasing.
1 Thessalonians 5:17

The next day Lori and I thought we could find a place between Limon and Littleton to park the trailer for the rest of the journey. When we knocked at the campground office in Limon, nobody answered. Then we drove down Highway 86 and wound up in Littleton where we still couldn't find a place. Then we drove to a KOA campground in Castle Rock, which was way out of our way, but it was closed for the winter.

The Elizabeth trailer park was full. Churches there and in Kiowa agreed to let us use their parking lot but had no hook up. We finally found, by the grace of God, an unadvertised RV hookup at the Kiowa fairgrounds. It was fifty miles from Limon *and* from Littleton. We decided to stay there the rest of the walk.

On Wednesday, November 17, Lori let me out of the truck where I had finished the previous day, and drove to Limon to wait for me by Interstate 70. That morning was so cold that my recorder kept messing up. It was thirty-five degrees with a light wind. But according to Colorado standards, the weather was excellent. They usually experienced a lot of snow and cold temperatures that time of year. As I headed for Limon, I could look east behind me and see relatively flat land, and west toward Limon and see scattered houses amongst the trees and the

117

snowcapped Rocky Mountains in the near distance. I would be climbing those mountains soon.

I had only walked a block when I heard a car behind me and turned around.

It was the guy in the maroon van.

A cold feeling erupted in my stomach but I continued walking. He must have been waiting for me to get out on the road. But waiting for what, I wondered. Or to do what? To harass me? To threaten or harm me?

Ahead several blocks, an old two-lane cement bridge with cement railings and narrow shoulders crossed a dry riverbed. A few trees sprinkled about the area, but the road in both directions was vacant.

The cold feeling in my stomach grew. I was out there alone and very vulnerable. I could feel my heart racing and my palms getting wet. I thought I would never see this guy again.

The van veered onto the shoulder directly behind me. I was walking facing traffic, so the guy had driven on the wrong side of the road to get there.

He was in the van by himself this time and he kept the motor running.

I continued to walk, looking behind me periodically.

The van sat still and the guy's mouth was moving. He was talking to himself.

What in the world was he doing, I wondered, both afraid and angry at the same time. Was he crazy? I didn't know what he was saying and I wasn't going to go back to find out. I turned to look at him again and slowed down. He motioned me to go on, then pulled out into the open short-grass field on the side of the road I was walking.

I kept going, with a funny feeling in my gut. I thought he was going to do something. I just didn't know what it was.

Suddenly the guy gunned the engine and the van plowed across the field almost fast enough to fishtail, kicking up dirt.

He drove a block or more away from me, between me and the bridge, and spun his van around facing me.

I didn't know what would happen next. My heart was in my throat.

Then the man jumped out of the van like he was in a hurry and stopped. He pointed his right arm at me with his left hand ten inches behind his right, extended as though to brace it. He had something in his right hand and spread his legs about three feet apart.

I had seen this stance a thousand times in the Army. It was a stance I was taught on the firing range shooting a pistol. I didn't actually see a gun, but I thought he had one, and he was going to shoot me.

Suddenly faith that could only have come from Christ filled me. I felt that peace that had only one great source.

And the peace of God, which surpasses all understanding, will keep your hearts and minds through Christ Jesus. (Phil. 4:7)

I prayed: "Lord, if it's my time, I am willing to give my life up."

The LORD is on my side;
I will not fear.
What can man do to me? (Ps. 118:6)

I walked the proudest that I had ever walked in my life. I was prepared to die to carry God's message to Columbine.

Suddenly cars appeared from both directions. I was so busy keeping an eye on that guy, and praying, that I didn't hear them until they were almost on me, but I was glad of it. When the cars started coming, the fellow put down his arm, jumped back into his van, and spun around in the field. The van fishtailed and threw up dirt and dust as it fled off the other way. I felt a wave of relief. In my heart I knew the guy wanted to shoot me.

No, I didn't see a gun for sure. But deep down I know what he intended to do. Once again God had sent His angels to surround me.

> *Keep me, O Lord, from the hands of the wicked;*
> *Preserve me from violent men,*
> *Who have purposed to make my steps stumble.* (Ps. 140:4)

I had met negative people on this walk, but this was the first time I met someone willing to kill because they hated what God stands for so much.

I walked into Limon, then rode around the town on I–70. When I thought about it, it seemed that the persecution from my family and friends, the lawmen in Kansas, the kids in Lamar, and that guy in the van had all come against me in different ways—my spirit, soul, and body—to stop my walk to Columbine. At any of those incidents I could have thrown my hands up and quit. I could also have quit because of my feet or because it was dangerous or because it was difficult. I understood on a different level what Paul meant when he said "fight the good fight of faith." I was in a spiritual fight and the battleground was not only my spirit but also my body and my mind.

When I told Lori what happened, she said, "God let me know that you would be safe. He won't let anybody harm you."

I believed that was true. Still, she seemed to keep more of an eye on me after that.

I started walking on Highway 86. On this side of Limon, there were many beautiful tall pine trees. It was a hilly area and green pancake-shaped cactus plants dotted the landscape. It was an old, well-used, two-lane road with plenty of asphalt patches and long jagged cracks. I could see straight ahead, almost due west, huge black mountains with snowcaps and large boulders. The sky was pretty and blue and many of the snowcaps reached into the clouds. A car passed me about every ten or fifteen minutes. I hoped the sign meant something to at least one of them.

If a person needed exercise, I would recommend walking along Highway 86. It's beautiful, quiet, and peaceful.

I figured it was going to be a slow day. Nobody could have stopped even if they wanted to because the road had only two lanes without enough shoulder for someone to pull off to the side. A person would have had to stop in the middle of the highway to talk to me. That could have been done, I guess, since there was so little traffic.

As I passed two houses, the first houses I had passed all day long, a woman driving a Volkswagen van in the direction I was headed stopped. She looked me over and frowned. "Do you want a ride to Kiowa?"

"I'm not taking rides. I'm walking all the way."

She nodded toward the mountain without taking her eyes off me. "You got a big sharp, heavy hill to climb," she said. "It's going to be very difficult."

I saw what she called a hill ahead of me, a mountain road that climbed at a thirty-five to forty degree angle. It was one massive rock with pine trees all over it and gray stone staring defiantly at me. I looked at her. "I'll make it one way or the other."

"God bless you," she said and went on her way.

I was eight miles from a town and only this woman and one other had stopped. One person had waved; perhaps as many as twenty cars had passed altogether. But these two were enough to cheer me up.

I looked at that sharp "hill." After walking a hundred yards or so, I realized what the lady had meant. In that area people called them steep hills. I called them mountains myself, being from Oklahoma. There were two of them. The first one went up a half mile and down a half mile. Then I had to climb the other hill, which was another mile. It would be especially hard to do while pulling the cross behind me.

As I started up, I told myself to take one step at a time. The right foot then the left slapped the pavement. One step at a time. Right, left. Right, left. Right, left. The wheel sang clinkety-clink, clinkety-clink, clinkety-clink. Right, left. Right, left. Right, left. Clinkety-clink, clinkety-clink, clinkety-clink. After the first quarter mile, my breathing deepened and I had to hold my mouth open to get enough air. Now I was deep into the incline and my rhythm changed. Right . . . push. Left . . . push. Right . . . push. Left . . . push. Clink . . . e . . . ty-clink, clink . . . e . . . ty-clink, clink . . . e . . . ty-clink. My heart was pumping hard now and I had started sweating all over again.

As I put weight on each leg, pain shot through my knees. As long as I had walked on level ground and moved my hips without moving my knees too much, I did fine. But climbing the hills forced me to put pressure on my knees.

My thighs began to burn. Two-thirds of the way up I started breathing heavily. Though winded, I was afraid to stop and rest. Sweat streamed into my eyes, down my cheeks and chin and dropped. Right . . . push. Left . . . push. Right . . . push. Left . . . push. Clink . . . e . . . ty-clink, clink . . . e . . . ty-clink, clink . . . e . . . ty-clink. The cross wheel rattled behind me against the silence of my surroundings. Every once in a while a bird chirped. One step at a time. Right . . . pull. Left . . . pull. Right . . . pull. Left . . . pull. I thought about riding up this monster in a car and the thought was pleasant. One step at a time. I was raining sweat now. Right . . . push. Left . . . push. Right . . . pull. Clink . . . e . . . ty-clink, clink . . . e . . . ty-clink. The cross had never seemed so heavy. I trudged on and stopped a moment and my thighs quivered from the exertion. The hill leveled out a bit, then dipped sharply and the next mountain ascended. It angled at about forty degrees with rocks beside the road as huge as I had ever seen.

It was a rough climb. I had a funny feeling the hills would get harder and harder. I started up the next one before I thought too long about it.

After I was over the second mountain, Lori came by and gave me a sandwich and a cold drink. I needed it, and the rest was good for my knees. After she went on, a man driving an old Ranger pickup pulled up. A very pleasant gentleman, he said, "I really want to encourage you for what you're doing."

I could tell the guy wasn't well off.

The man held out a bunch of coins in a change purse. "That's the only money I've got. I want to give it to you."

The purse was like one my grandpa had used. Usually when somebody offered money, I took it because I knew they were doing something for the Lord. I believed the Lord always paid them back and much more and in more ways than I ever could, but this time I refused. I told him, "The Lord's taking care of me. We're doing fine."

"Well, that's all I have. If you want it you can take it."

I didn't. That was one time I think the Lord wanted me to refuse a gift. He was glad I didn't take it, I thought. It may have been all the money he had to his name and I didn't want it.

At the top of one mountain, I saw huge Rockies around Castle Rock, which was to the west. The clouds were very white and a beautiful stream snaked along pine trees, boulders, and small rocks. The red and purple wildflowers were everywhere. It was a beautiful snowcapped sight, but I hoped the mountain didn't get any more snow on it until Monday evening. I was approaching Kiowa, and from there to Littleton was fifty miles. I was close. The thought of it sent chills through my body. I would reach Columbine in a couple of days if things went right. If we did, I would leave Littleton for Oklahoma City on Monday around noon. So if it snowed on the mountains Monday evening, that would be fine and dandy with me.

When the sun began falling below the top of the mountains, darkness came on quickly. The wind was blowing out of the south, which would keep things warm. This would fool the weathermen, who had predicted temperatures in the thirties.

More frequently now, since I was nearing a more populated

area, people drove by, and waved, and gave me the thumbs-up. It seemed like a car drove by every fifteen seconds or so, encouraging me. It made all the difference in the world.

Behind all that encouragement, a group of high school boys drove by in a white mid-'90s Chevrolet and flashed me a hand sign that young gang members use. I guessed they had just gotten out of school.

I stuck my finger straight up in the air and said, "Praise the Lord."

At the end of that day, I had almost walked thirty miles through the mountains. That was hard to believe, but I was getting close and the adrenaline was beginning to work on me.

Before going to bed that night, I heard a discussion on KHOW's "The Reggie Rivers Show" on the radio out of Denver.

One person asked where God was during the Columbine shooting. Another asked why God wasn't there, if there was one. I called the show, got on, and told them about my walk to Columbine.

Rivers, who was very professional and was trying to remain neutral, asked, "Do you believe walking 700 miles will do any good?"

"It will do what God wants it to do."

"Are you telling us that this is a mission from God?"

"Yes. I suspect most of your listeners won't understand that."

"Have you faced any trouble on the highway?"

"I've been put to the test several times and the Lord has always helped me through."

One caller said, "I believe the Bible is just a story book that someone wrote. It isn't true."

That statement upset me a little. I said, "The Bible is the truth, and you can count on standing in front of God one of these days."

I answered questions for a good twenty minutes. I was on so long because I got callers talking about religion. There couldn't have been a single Christian that called among the bunch. One asked if I was crazy, another asked whether I had nothing else to do with my life, more than one called the Bible a "story," and several said prayer was a waste of time. I had never heard so many people who didn't believe in the Bible and people who believed it was a myth in all my life.

I know everybody wasn't that way in Denver, but most of the callers to that show were. I didn't know what to think. Hearing all that godlessness depressed me. I told Lori later if it wasn't for the Lord wanting me to do this, I would have packed up and gone home that very night.

But she said, "You've come too far to quit now."

Although I had only recently accepted Christ, I had always believed He existed. I wondered if I had not had prayer when I attended school, would I have been like some of the callers? I was being naïve, I knew, but it was hard for me to comprehend so many people not believing in God, even being outright hostile to God.

That night I thought about how many people hated God— and allowed that one radio show to upset me too much. Their godless attitude confirmed for me that we would run into trouble at Columbine, not serious trouble but a lot of negativity. Everything wouldn't go right at the finish. I didn't want to cause any trouble; I only wanted to publicize the importance of getting prayer back in schools.

The next morning, November 18, when I left the Kiowa fairgrounds, the wind was blowing from the north at about thirty-five miles an hour and it was around forty degrees. The wind chill made it feel like the coldest morning of the trip. After an hour of walking, traffic seemed to double, with cars passing every few seconds. The wind had increased to fifty miles an hour and the temperature dropped ten or fifteen degrees.

As I yelled above the wind into the recorder, a 1988 light blue Ford sedan with a long scrape on the driver's side came up the hill and headed for me.

Standing on the edge of the pavement, I looked up and got a flash of white hair and glasses peering through the top of the steering wheel. I thought the car would veer toward the lane, which was clear, but it rushed dead at me. A chill shot right up my spine and for a brief moment I was frozen, starring back at the approaching sedan.

Oh, Lord. I thought I was a dead man.

Instinctively, I pitched the cross aside and dove for the ditch.

The car roared over the spot where I had been standing, the wind fluttered grass in its wake. I rolled to my knees on the side of the ditch and saw the cross for a brief moment at the edge of the road. It looked undamaged. Breathing deeply, my heart thundered in my chest as I watched the car drive off. The woman looked about eighty-five years old, and she had had to swerve onto the shoulder to get to me. I was relieved enough to be mad.

I mean she just about got me! Another two inches and she would have! I tried to calm my nerves and got to my feet. I still had the recorder in my hand. My heart was still pounding and in my mind I could see that car coming at me.

It was a scary feeling, even after it was over. I dusted myself off and picked up the cross, which was still in one piece.

After that, I walked on the sandy part of the road. She hadn't tried to hit me on purpose, I was sure; she was just elderly and didn't see me.

Soon after that, Lori came by. We screamed to hear each other over the wind, which rocked the truck.

Lori said, "The weatherman said the wind's at seventy miles an hour and it's about to blow the trailer over."

She was trying to get me to quit for that day.

"It's blowing too bad for you to walk."

But it was only 9:30 in the morning so I still had several good hours left. I wanted to get as close to Littleton as I could, but the closer I got, the harder the walk was getting. Shaking my head, I said, "If it gets colder with a seventy mile-an-hour wind, it will be worse than it is now. I want to walk as long as I can before that happens."

"I thought that's what you would say," Lori said, "so I got you an egg sandwich and orange juice so at least you could eat something!"

I ate quickly and got back on the road. Up higher now I could see houses built on the mountainside amongst pine trees. The higher I got the fiercer the wind blew, whisking smoke from chimneys sideways, swaying electric lines back and forth. Like a hand it shoved me, plastered my clothes against me, and nearly knocked me over. It whined and roared so loudly that I couldn't hear cars until they were twenty yards in front of me. As I walked, I wrapped my left arm around the cross and held it down with my right hand to keep it from blowing away. When I headed west the wind pushed the cross sideways. I fought just to put one foot in front of another and bowed my head into the gust to keep the wind and dust out of my eyes.

When I took one of my gloves off, the wind whipped it so far away so fast that I couldn't chase it down. When my other glove flew out of my back pocket, I didn't bother to go after it. Everything I didn't have strapped down, the wind swept away.

Through it all, I still felt an adrenaline rush. That, I think, and God were the only things that kept me fighting the wind.

I was almost run over again when one car passed another one and nearly plowed into me. At the time, I hadn't been paying attention and had gotten too close to the road. I didn't hear the car until it was a few yards away.

At one point a carload of kids came by with their windows rolled down. One light haired girl stuck her head out the window. She pointed and laughed at me and screamed. "Look at the crazy old man."

The wind howled so loudly that I could hear little else she

said. Even though I now expected the ridicule, it still hurt when it happened. I was carrying the cross for those kids, and it was pretty discouraging and depressing to be treated that way. I really began to look forward to finishing the walk.

It was hard for me to keep a good attitude. I realized God had to pitch in and help me do that mentally because I couldn't do it myself. When I reached the top of the hill, I got down on my knees beside the road and prayed. "Give me the mental strength to handle the wind," I said. "I pray for better weather. Fill me with the Holy Spirit. Let me continue my walk under a better mental attitude. Lord, I thank you for getting us this far. Give me the strength mentally to make it as you have given me the strength physically. Lord, change my attitude. God, you can heal my knees if you will. In Jesus' name, I pray, amen."

After praying, I felt much better, physically and mentally. I thought about how Jesus, especially while He was carrying His cross, had to endure much more than I had from unbelievers: they spat on Him, made fun of Him, and cursed Him.

> But they cried out, "Away with Him, away with Him! Crucify Him!"
> Pilate said to them, "Shall I crucify your King?"
> The chief priests answered, "We have no king but Caesar!" (John 19:15)

I wasn't comparing myself to Jesus in any way. My own suffering only gave me a small taste of what He had experienced. Maybe I needed that. Maybe that was why the Lord told me to carry the cross. A few minutes after I prayed, the wind died down to five or ten miles an hour and people were driving by honking and waving. Some may say that it just happened, but I truly believe God took control of the wind.

> But He said to them, "Where is your faith?"
> And they were afraid, and marveled, saying to one another, "Who can this be? For He commands even the winds and water, and they obey Him!" (Luke 8:25)

Elias was a man with a nature like ours, and he prayed earnestly that it would not rain; and it did not rain on the land for three years and six months. (James 5:17)

Shortly thereafter I walked through Elizabeth, a small town with old brick buildings on each side of the main street for a block or more. I saw a small restaurant and I purchased a soda at a convenience store, then got back on the road. Highway 86 outside Elizabeth was still two lanes with a three-foot wide shoulder made of gravel.

A woman mail carrier, driving one of those United States Postal Service Jeeps with the steering wheel on the wrong side, stopped me outside town. "Where are you going and where did you come from?"

"I'm from Oklahoma City and I'm headed for Columbine High School."

She said, "That's cool. Are you hungry? If you are, I'll get you something to eat."

She would have had to stop delivering her mail and fallen behind her schedule if she went back to Elizabeth. I couldn't believe she had offered, and she was serious about it. It made me feel bad about my own poor attitude. I was bouncing up when something good happened and falling flat when something bad happened, like I was on an emotional roller coaster. This was partly because I felt more strongly than ever that prayer had to be in schools, partly because I was struggling to walk through a pretty tough stretch, but mainly because I hadn't matured enough to handle it. I thought God was showing me that I needed to get my priorities in the right place and stop blaming other people for how I felt. "Thanks," I told her, "but my wife is following me with something to eat."

"I'm really, really proud of what you're doing," she said, and drove on.

The prayer, the dying wind, and the mail carrier put me in a better mood.

At this location the pine trees were thick and fifty feet tall or more, so, even at noon, I could hardly see the sun. Reddish brown pine needles carpeted the ground all around me. As I walked along, I spotted a Sears charge card and picked it up to return to the owners. It appeared fairly new. I also found an envelope addressed to the parents of a student at Elizabeth High School, and I figured it was a report card. When I got to a mailbox later that day, I dropped it in. I thought that kid might not be very happy about his report card showing up.

My attitude had improved so much after the mail carrier stopped that I grinned and waved at every car that passed. More than half of them waved back. I could tell that a lot of them didn't want to, but I didn't care. I kept on doing it.

I had had a pretty good walk going down a mountain for the last fifteen minutes. I kept catching myself almost jogging. I was about thirty miles from Littleton. The adrenaline had kicked in really big. My feet weren't hurting and I was bending my knees, which I hadn't been doing before. I kept thinking that at this pace I would burn myself out and never make it and tried to slow myself down.

If I could get to Parker, about thirteen miles away, I realized, I could make it to Columbine High School the next day. The very thought excited me.

In Franktown, a city of a little over 5,000 people, I saw a lumberyard and a strip of one-story office buildings. I was entering a more populated area and traffic was steady. Five blocks ahead I would turn on Highway 83 and walk north to Parker. I quickly ate lunch with Lori in town and headed toward Parker, nine miles away now. I had already made sixteen miles. It was around 2:30 P.M. and I would make Parker even if I had to walk in the dark.

When a Colorado State trooper passed me and spun around, I was headed north out of Franktown on a two-lane highway. I got that nervous feeling in my stomach again and braced myself. I thought I had seen the end of them.

The patrolman stopped in front of me and got out. He was smiling, which calmed me some, and extended his hand. "I've been following you since before Limon," he said. "I want to say God bless you, sir. I appreciate so much what you're trying to do. I have informed your daughter Ammie daily about how you were doing."

I was touched by his kindness. He had gone out of his way to give Ammie a daily report on my progress, probably through contacting law enforcement agencies along my route. This man was truly his brother's keeper and I was very proud to be his brother. I said, "I appreciate your concern for me."

We hugged each other.

The Spirit of the Lord came over me and I started crying. I was ashamed for judging all police as bad when there had only been a few with bad attitudes. Most of them were good people. It was a good lesson that God had taught me: let Him judge people; I should concentrate on loving them. In my mind I asked God to forgive me for judging all for what a few had done.

At Franktown, I called Evan Dryer at the *Denver Post.* "I won't call another newspaper if you do a good story on me," I told him. "I *will* call one or two television stations to do a story."

"Oh, I'll do a good story on you," Dryer said. "I promise you that."

The story of the walk had grown after the Associated Press reported it. I felt I could have had every newspaper and television station in Denver and the surrounding areas waiting at Columbine to cover the story. I only had been two miles from the Murrah building in Oklahoma City when the bomb went off and knew one of the people who had died. I also had worked on a house that had been struck by the May 3, 1999, tornado in Oklahoma City. I knew several people who had lost their houses and everything in them in that terrible storm. I had seen what these disasters had done and how the media descended on the scene. I didn't know what Columbine folks were going through, but I knew about all the news coverage Oklahoma City had received. I figured if I could get a handful of the larger news outlets rather all the every news agency to cover us, I wouldn't cause a big scene at the school.

Dryer gave me the name of the church the Bernalls attended so I would know where to take the Bible.

In the next few miles Highway 83 turned into six lanes into Parker and I was walking on a six-foot cement shoulder. Parker was elevated and I could see the suburbs of Denver. It was just getting dark and I saw houses, apartment buildings, skyscrapers, the lights along the interstate, and the snowcapped mountains in the background. It was a huge beautiful city at night.

I paused a moment, if not in my step in my mind, to stare down there, knowing that somewhere was Columbine High School.

What a feeling! It was incredible!

In less than twenty miles my journey would be over. I had almost made it. I gave thanks to God for getting Lori and me there safely.

Lori had gone ahead to Parker. When I got there, we would drive to Littleton to see the condition of the road and decide if I really could make it the following day.

I had walked until six o'clock, almost thirty miles—*five miles past Parker!*

Unbelievable!

Chapter Fourteen
Columbine

And let us not grow weary while doing good,
for in due season we shall reap if we do not lose heart.
Galatians 6:9

On the last day of the walk, we were up at 4:30 getting our showers and doctoring my feet. It was still dark when we left Kiowa and drove to where I had finished the day before.

I left at 6:30 in the morning on Friday, November 19, sixteen miles from Columbine High School, which was on the southern edge of Denver. It was about forty-five degrees that morning and the sun was shining, but the conditions were insignificant. I was convinced that I would make it easily. I felt like I had the strength of ten men. I felt like Samson that day. I was full of the Holy Spirit. I could tell because I didn't have any pains in my body. My feet weren't hurting. Nothing was going to stop me.

Before I left I called a television station and Evan Dryer at the *Denver Post*. I agreed to call Dryer back when I was thirty minutes from the high school.

I moved almost at a jog, and I kept slowing myself down. When Lori called to say she would be waiting for me at one place, I would have already passed it.

About three hours after I started, I turned on Arapahoe Road and entered Littleton, a clean busy city with many office buildings and apartments. It reminded me of downtown Guthrie,

Oklahoma, with a lot of people on the sidewalks and a lot of his-
toric looking buildings. It was a pleasant touristy town. The
traffic was thick, six to eight lanes of bumper to bumper auto-
mobiles headed for work. I walked past Newton Middle School
and headed north on Broadway. When I got to Littleton Avenue,
I had seven miles to go.

Several people downtown hollered, "God bless you"; others
said, "Keep going."

With four miles to go, close enough for me to reach the school
by 1:30 that day, I stopped at a sandwich shop where I would
meet Lori for lunch. I called two television stations and the
Denver Post, which sent out a reporter, whom we waited for.

Lori didn't tell me that Windie and Ammie were on their way
to meet me before I completed the walk; she wanted to surprise me with that news. When I found out, I realized that it
would take them an hour and a half to catch up with me. That
created a slight problem because I had told the television stations that I would reach the school in forty-five minutes. If I
kept to the television and newspaper schedule, I would have
to continue on right away. But if my daughters were going to
see me carrying the cross, I needed to wait.

I made a choice. I thanked God that Windie and Ammie were
going to be there, and I wanted them there with me during the
last mile. It meant more to me for them to see me carrying the
cross than all the media coverage I could get. I thought this
might encourage them in their faith.

The *Denver Post* reporter arrived before Lori and I finished
eating. He and I sat on the tailgate of my truck for half an hour
while he interviewed me.

After spending another forty-five minutes at the restaurant,
I set out again. I tried to record my feelings on my tape player,
but I was crying too much. It was one of the most emotional
times in my life. The Lord had said go and we had, and now I
was on the brink of completing the mission He had given me.
Despite the hernias and bad knees and blistered feet we had

made it. The grind of walking 700 miles began and was ending one step at a time. I hadn't known if I could do it physically, I hadn't known if someone wouldn't attack me on the highway, and I didn't see a way to do it financially. I had expected the tough physical part, but the spiritual and mental struggle with the persecution had made me think about quitting. God and Lori and people we ministered to had kept me going during those times. I believe I had grown as a person and for sure as a child of God. I felt like He would be proud of me for doing it and I was also proud of myself. I felt Lori would be proud that we had made the trip.

I saw tears in Lori's eyes as she watched me begin the last four miles. God had brought us closer together during the walk. She had taken insults about herself and me from people to get here and stood by me all of the way. Thank God. She would be at the finish line waiting on me.

At 2:10, thirty-five more minutes before the walk would end, I was still unable to record my feelings without breaking down.

An air horn tooted behind me, and somebody yelled, "Dad!"

I looked around to see my daughter and son-in-law's large motor home. Windie and Ammie stuck their heads out one of the windows.

My heart jumped. They had made it.

The girls waved and drove on ahead to Clement Park, which was near Columbine High School.

A few minutes later Lori met me in the pickup and let both girls out. Physically, Windie and Ammie were like carbon copies of each other: light brown hair, thin and very pretty. Windie, the older by a year, had the hotter temper. Ammie tended to be very sincere. One wore blue jeans and the other had on black pants.

They were going to walk with me, I realized. I didn't think I could heave been more full of joy, but having them walk with me was more than I had hoped for.

Both girls were crying and both hugged me at the same time.

I really started crying then. I never would have dreamed that carrying the cross would have made us closer as a family, but it had, and it had brought my whole family closer to Christ. Windie and Ammie shared the success of carrying the cross with us.

"I'm real proud of you," one of them said.

"Yes, we're real proud of you," the other said.

"Are you tired?" Ammie asked.

"No," I said, "I'm not tired. I feel real good."

I felt like a proud hen as she walks with her chicks. I considered that this might be the major thing Windie and Ammie would remember about me after I was gone. And, hopefully, they will pass the story on to my grandchildren.

One of my daughters walked on each side of me. I was in a residential area by then, Bowles Street, with a sidewalk about four feet wide. I noticed a lot of American flags, four-lane streets, six feet adobe fences, a lot of evergreens, and very green grass. Most of the houses were brick and many were two stories tall. I could also see what looked like townhouses and condominiums.

As the girls held my arm, they waved to the people who were honking, cheering, and giving the thumbs-up sign.

I turned south off Bowles onto South Pierce Street, the street in front of Columbine High School. Clement Park, which was a green blanket of grass and large trees, was beside me and I could see the school, a two-level adobe colored building, a few blocks away.

Lori and the *Denver Post* reporter who had interviewed me at the sandwich shop were waiting for us at Clement Park. Lori grabbed my arm and I kissed her.

Ahead, I saw parents in cars lining the street waiting to pick up their children, a steady stream of cars leaving with their children, and students coming out of the high school. I could see one parking lot on the southeast edge of the school and others on the north and west sides.

I had arrived at Columbine High School at 2:45, which was when it dismissed. If I had known that Columbine let out then, I wouldn't have arrived at that time. I should have known this, especially with all the time I had walking to think about it. Because of all the trouble the school had had, I wanted to respect the students. My plans were to carry the cross on the sidewalk in front of the school, give my story to any reporters and then return to the park with the cross. But when I had to wait for Windie and Ammie to get there I didn't think through how that would change when I got to the high school. Hindsight is perfect, but that's the problem with it. It's hindsight.

Although it was the wrong time to get there, parents going and coming continued honking and waving as they drove by me. News people were setting up cameras on the sidewalk in front of the school and they were already shooting me as I walked down the last two blocks. Students and parents were trying to see what was going on.

As I walked the last few yards, a student about sixteen years old drove by us in an '80s model brown Toyota pickup with a camper shell on it. When he saw me carrying the cross, he flipped me off.

It was a mean thing to do and could start the kind of trouble I wanted to avoid. I kept going, halfway ignoring him and hoping he would go on about his business. Students were all over the sidewalk now, walking on the grass as they went to their cars and waited for parents to pick them up.

But he made a U-turn and came back.

No! What was he going to do?

As he drove by, he scowled at me and screamed at the top of his lungs, "Go home!" Then he cursed my daughters and me as he pointed a finger at us. Then he yelled at the news people, "No more cameras!"

I felt myself deflating. This was the last thing I wanted to happen. I was glad it was almost over. Ten minutes before I had been higher than I had ever been in my life. Now it was hard to stay up mentally. My daughters had driven 700 miles to see me go through this. Just then, the Lord told me not to say anything and I told my daughters to keep quiet. As I kept walking toward the school, I tried to tune out everybody except my family.

The student in the Toyota pickup pulled up halfway on the grass and ran inside the school.

I had no idea what he was going to do, but I figured it was bad. I kept walking, working my way through the students on the sidewalk.

Then the student who had flipped me off rushed out of the school like he was going to put out a fire. Several other students, school officials, and a security guard were behind him, running too.

I knew I had to keep my focus. I told Windie and Ammie, "Don't put your feet on school property."

The kid headed straight for me, and Windie, the hotter tempered one, stepped around me as though to get between me and the student.

He stopped a yard from me and cursed up a red storm.

"Don't say anything," I told Windie, as I tried to ignore the kid. I kept walking.

The school security guard stopped at the sidewalk where I was walking. Lori and the *Denver Post* reporter were a few feet behind me, along with my son-in-law and grandson.

I was in front of the school by then and had only to walk a few more yards. Camera crews continued to take pictures.

While some school officials and teachers watched what was going on, other teachers, students, and a security guard put their hands over several TV camera lenses. The security guard ordered, "Get off school property."

"We're not on school property," one of the cameramen replied and removed the man's hand. "We're on the sidewalk."

The traffic was hardly moving because parents arriving and

leaving were still honking and waving at me. If nothing else, I thought, they all got to read the sign.

The news people videotaped the bad actions of the students and school officials, and the story went nationwide—on CNN and in *USA Today*. They didn't pick up the good stuff. It didn't make us look bad; it made the school look bad.

I walked to the far end of the school building, crossed the street, and walked back even with the school.

I was finished. I had completed my walk to Columbine, but I felt a long way from celebrating.

While I was finishing, Lori told me later, two boys and a girl wearing a Cassie Bernall tee shirt told her that a boy was going to bomb our pickup. She ran to the truck, which was in a nearby parking lot off school property. There, several high school boys were throwing soda cans at the pickup.

Lori treated them like a mother would a child, she said, and told them, "This is not necessary; I'll move the truck." She really didn't know how the students would react, but they said nothing and walked away.

Eager to get out of there, I was on my way to load the cross in the truck when I overheard a television reporter ask Ammie, "What did you think of your Dad walking 700 miles to deliver a message of peace to Columbine?"

"I can't believe how some of the students treated my dad," she said. "After the bombing in Oklahoma City, we had people come from Colorado to help us. We held our hands out in love and accepted their help. My dad put on hold a twenty-two-year-old business and walked 700 miles to show his love for the students and families who have suffered in this shooting. Then he gets treated like this. I just can't believe it."

I tapped her on the leg. "It's okay. Don't worry about it."

The reporter turned to my other daughter. "What do you think about it?"

"My family is getting ready to move to Colorado," she said,

"and it is going to be hard on me to do that after the way Dad was treated."

I knew that my daughters wanted to say a lot more but held back, and I was proud of them for restraining themselves.

"Would you do it again?" the reporter asked me.

"I don't know what the aftermath of the walk will be, but God knows and He knows how many people the walk touched. If God asked me to walk again I would."

"Do you think God is pleased with you?"

"I think that God is looking down at me smiling, and I hope He is saying, 'Well done my good and faithful servant.' "

Afterward, I loaded up the cross and my daughters left. My mission was not finished that day. I was ready to go home, but I still had to get the Bible to the Bernalls. I was mentally torn up because of the way the walk ended. After that, I didn't want to take the Bible to the Bernalls. I just wanted to go on home to Oklahoma City and cover my head up. But the next morning Lori insisted that I finish what I had started. So we drove to South Sheraton Baptist Church where they were presenting the play, *The Cassie Bernall Story*.

There, we gave the Bible to the youth pastor, Jason Janz, for the Bernalls, who agreed to see that they got it. I also gave him the sign from the back of the cross: "GOD WANTS <u>PRAYER</u> BACK IN SCHOOL." He wanted us to watch the play and for me to say a few words, but mentally I couldn't handle it.

Exhausted and upset after walking 700 miles, now I was wondering if I had done it all for nothing. The negative reaction of the Columbine High School officials and students was the finish I had hoped wouldn't come. School leaders, I am sure, knew we were on a mission to encourage prayer in school. Some people may disagree with prayer, but how many would say it's bad? None of the school administrators, teachers or security people made a move to respect God and prayer, and their lack of action taught those kids not to respect God.

In hindsight, I realize they did only what was in their hearts.

As the Lord has shown me since then, there in their hearts lay the real trouble with our public school system. He also showed me how to return prayer to public school in spite of it.

Chapter Fifteen
Every Child Covered

"If My people who are called by My name will humble themselves, and pray and seek My face, and turn from their wicked ways, then I will hear from heaven, and will forgive their sin and heal their land."

2 Chronicles 7:14

For two months after the walk, my faith was at a low point. The ridicule in Lamar, the guy in the maroon van, and the chaos at Columbine High School were hard to get over. Before I gave my life to the Lord, I had always been in control of what happened and I was very impatient. So much of what I experienced on the walk was out of my control and things got out of hand. It was hard for me to see the good over the bad. A more mature Christian may not have missed a beat, but I wasn't that mature regarding people who hate God.

I couldn't see how they could hate Jesus so much.

Perhaps I was experiencing what Elijah had experienced after he defeated the prophets of Baal. He had accomplished a great feat with God's power behind him. After he won, he became depressed and hid in a cave for a while. I had actually done what I set out to do, certainly with God's help. But I was so up emotionally, with the adrenaline rush working in me for two or three days straight, that when I came down I fell as low as I had been high.

I tried to make sense of what had happened. While I had succeeded in obeying God, obviously I had moved in zeal, perhaps without the knowledge I needed. Yet God honored my obedience.

I didn't consider that God is always on time even when we think He is late. But it is His time, not Garlin Newton's.

Although I continued to appear on TV and radio shows talking about the walk and encouraging a return of prayer to schools, I couldn't shake my disappointment and frustration. My faith just couldn't get right for some reason.

Then I remembered Luke 22:31–32.

> *And the Lord said, "Simon, Simon! Indeed, Satan has asked for you, that he may sift you as wheat. But I have prayed for you, that your faith should not fail; and when you have returned to Me, strengthen your brethren."*

That was happening to me. Satan was trying to destroy my faith. I got on my knees at the horse stable and prayed like never before. I asked Jesus to pray for me.

I had known Jesus as Savior. I had accepted Him as Lord. I had walked with Him as Provider. I had experienced Him as Protector. I had depended on Him as Strengthener. Now I met Him as Intercessor.

> *Therefore He is also able to save to the uttermost those who come to God through Him, since He always lives to make intercession for them.* (Heb. 7:25)

The next day I started getting strong in faith and rededicated myself to God and was ready to do whatever He wanted me to do again. I was on fire for the Lord and wanted to get Bearing the Cross Ministry going.

About two days later, February 20, 2000, a *Denver Post* article, consuming about three-quarters of the front page, discussed getting prayer and the Ten Commandments back in school.

The article, written by Kevin Simpson, said:

"When Garlin Newton walked from his Oklahoma City home to Columbine High School in November, shouldering a cross and a sign reading, 'God wants prayer back in school,' he unwittingly launched a road-side referendum."

I saw then how much of an impact the walk had made.

That article and other articles discussed the pros and cons of returning prayer to schools and the difficulty in doing so. The truth is parents, school administrators, and legislatures will argue this issue until the cows come home—and do nothing, or fix it in such a way that it's worse than it is now.

God can return to the classroom in spite of the continuing argument and I'm going to show you how. First, here's Scripture that I believe illustrates the current spiritual state of our public school system. It's Psalm 80: 8–13:

You have brought a vine out of Egypt;
You have cast out the nations, and planted it.
You prepared room for it,
And caused it to take deep root,
And it filled the land.
The hills were covered with its shadow,
And the mighty cedars with its boughs.
She sent out her boughs to the Sea,
And her branches to the River.
Why have You broken down her hedges,
So that all who pass by the way pluck her fruit?
The boar out of the wood uproots it,
And the wild beast of the field devours it.

Bible scholars have applied these verses to Israel and the church. Let's look at what it means. While Israel came out of Egypt literally, Christians come out of Egypt (a kind of slavery to sin) symbolically. Israel entered Canaan, filled the area and began influencing the world for God; Christians enter their Canaan, where God rules, and change lives. Then Israel turned from God and enemies began destroying them. When a Christian turns from Christ, he opens a door for Satan to attack him, and destroy him, if he could.

I want to apply these verses to our public school system. Men and women who wanted to freely worship the God of the Bible settled this country. They declared in The Constitution that the country would uphold religious freedoms. From religious groups came our school system, a successful system that publicly and freely honored God. When we honored God, He gave us wisdom to use the knowledge we learned in classrooms. I believe this wisdom was behind our ending slavery, our granting the right to vote to women, and our success against our military enemies. As well, the inventions and discoveries that have come out of the United States have totally changed life for the better around the world.

But now we have "broken down her hedges." The hedge of God, the Ten Commandments and prayer, was our protection. When we reinterpreted our laws, we took God out of our classrooms and removed His protection. The righteousness of God has been like a fence around a house, allowing a child to play anywhere inside, protected from the dangers of the streets, traffic, or evil people. Psalm 11:3 asks:

> *If the foundations are destroyed,*
> *What can the righteous do?*

The foundation of our public school system, honoring God, has been destroyed. So what can the righteous do? We must rebuild the foundation by covering every child in America with prayer. And I have a personal testimony proving how well it can work.

I found out almost a year after I carried the cross to Columbine that prayer in school played a critical part in my salvation.

I attended grade school several years with a girl named Linda, who was from a good Christian family. Her mother warned her not to have anything to do with me because my family life didn't reflect Christian values. Then I went one way and she went the other and I didn't see or hear from her for thirty-eight years. When Linda read about one of my upcoming walks in her local newspaper, she called me. She was excited that I was not only saved but also carrying a cross for the Lord. She said she had been praying for me to get saved—since the third grade. For thirty-eight years she had prayed for me in.

While our children now won't be exposed to God or the Ten Commandments or prayer in school, we can cover them, administrators, and employees with prayer just like Linda covered me. We can pray God's protection over them and that their hearts will become soft toward Him for salvation.

To this end, the Lord has prompted me to establish a program, part of Bearing the Cross Ministry, called Every Child Covered. Every Child Covered is dedicated to covering every child in America with prayer.

God is waiting to hear from you and me. 2 Chronicles 7:14 says:

> *"If My people who are called by My name will humble themselves, and pray and seek My face, and turn from their wicked ways, then I will hear from heaven, and will forgive their sin and heal their land."*

Prayer cover worked for me, and it will influence millions of children in this country. God wants to bless them and save them for an eternal relationship with Him.

For Every Child Covered™ to work, we need Christians from all over the United States committing to pray for specific individuals.

I don't know all the ways this can be done. But one way is for a family to accumulate a written list of children and their family members from their neighborhood or apartment complex. Your children will know who the other children are in the area, so you won't have to force prayer down any child's throat. The child might not even know you are praying for them.

You and your children can then pray over the list of names as the Lord leads you.

For sure you would pray for each child's safety, for their salvation, that they would learn and enjoy school, that each child discovers God's purpose for their lives, for their parents, siblings, friends and even pets.

Your church or intercessory prayer group may want to become involved. A family that homeschools their children could be particularly effective prayer warriors in Every Child Covered.

Bearing the Cross Ministry

Bearing the Cross Ministry was birthed when the Lord spoke to my spirit: "You are going to have a ministry called Bearing the Cross Ministry. You will give testimonies anywhere you can to draw attention to getting prayer back in school."

My life has been greatly fulfilled since the Lord called me to carry the cross. The Lord chooses where I walk. As I carry the cross, I pray for people, give my testimony, lead people to the Lord, preach at churches, and speak at schools.

When I look back on carrying that cross 700 miles, I remember the physical, emotional, and spiritual effort it took. The most fulfilling part, though, was ministering to people on the roadside and going to churches and giving my testimony. It was a different way of life for me, and one I never thought I would enjoy, but I did. When I carried the cross, I felt closer to God than I had ever felt in my life. I felt alive. My life seems empty when I'm not carrying the cross.

When you are on a mission for God, I learned, it's one of the best times of your life. You will do things that seem impossible, but you will find that all things are possible with Him.

A few weeks after the walk I noticed that my knees weren't hurting and took one of the braces off for a day and felt no pain. Two days later I took the other one off. Since then I have not worn either brace or even taken an aspirin. The Lord healed my knees.

Lori has a testimony as well. Her hands gradually began clearing up for two or three days after I prayed for them but she didn't say anything. She thought it might have been because of a change in climates. She didn't know I had prayed for her hands until we were on our way back to Oklahoma and heard me pray for them on tape.

"Several months later, I knew my hands were better and kept in mind that Garlin had prayed for them," she said. "I didn't mention it to anyone because I wanted to be sure! It was not an instant healing. Finally, I told Garlin and thanked God. Now after a year and a half, my hands are still doing well."

Every Child Covered

If you decide to participate in Every Child Covered, will you contact Bearing the Cross Ministry?

Write to:

Bearing the Cross Ministry
P.O. Box 13282
Oklahoma City, OK 73114

Or email:

garlinnewton@aol.com

Exciting Titles from **The Colbert House!**

Songs of Zion
A novel by Larry L. Colbert

The Gestapo hunts a Jewess who has the stolen relic that Adolf Hitler believes gives him the power to rule the world.

World War II provides the setting for fast-paced suspense, romance, and living faith. Readers who like an intriguing story and history that leaps off the page will find this book enjoyable.

"It is a hard book to put down."—*The Sunday Oklahoman*

"I just finished reading *Songs of Zion* and I absolutely love it!"—JB from IL

ISBN: 1—887399—03—8, 448 pp., hardback, $23.99

Unhandcuffing God
A book for victorious living by Howard Caver

You can experience miracles in your life!

Howard Caver shares how God performed miracles for him, his family, and the church he pastors "beyond what he could ask or think."

For pastors of small congregations, small para-church ministries, and individuals called to do more than they have resources to do.

ISBN: 1—887399—07-0, 160 pp., paper, $10.99

Dance Before the Lord
A book on spiritual warfare by Ron Dryden.

Learn to dance in praise to overcome persecution, initiate deliverance, strengthen marriages, and develop greater fellowship with Christ. Provides an in-depth study of this powerful spiritual weapon.

"I Heartily recommend . . . this great accounting of God's power in the dance." Dr. John Avanzini, host of TBN's "Principles of Biblical Economics" Program.

ISBN: 1—887399—00-3, 160 pp., paper, $9.95

33 Truths You Should Know About Jesus and the Cross
A book on the basics of Christianity by Larry L. Colbert.

Centered on Jesus' redemptive work, this book presents basic Christianity and difficult Bible concepts in everyday terms. Designed to be studied quickly, it provides Scripture references for deeper study.

ISBN: 1—887399—04-6, 64 pp., paper, $4.95

ORDER FORM

FAX (405) 329-6977

Phone Toll-free 1-800-698-2644 with a credit card

Postal The Colbert House, P.O. Box 150, Norman, OK 73070-0150 USA

Please send the following books
I understand that I may return any book for a full refund.

❏ *Carrying the Cross to Columbine* by Garlin Newton, 160 pp., paper, $10.99

❏ *Songs of Zion* by Larry L. Colbert, 448 pp., hardback, $23.99

❏ *Unhandcuffing God* by Howard Caver, 160 pp., paper, $10.99

❏ *Dance Before the Lord* by Ron Dryden,160 pp., paper, $9.95.

❏ *33 Truths You Should Know About Jesus and the Cross* by Larry L. Colbert, 64 pp., paper, $4.95

Book Title	No. of Copies	Subtotal

Sales tax: Oklahoma residents please add 7.5% _____

Shipping: Free _____

                                        TOTAL _____

Payment:
Check/money order ❏ VISA ❏ Mastercard ❏ American Express
Card Number _____

Name on Card _____ Exp. date _____

Name _____

Address _____

City _____ State _____ Zip _____

Phone _____

Thank you for your order!

ORDER FORM

FAX (405) 329-6977

Phone Toll-free 1-800-698-2644 with a credit card

Postal The Colbert House, P.O. Box 150, Norman, OK 73070-0150 USA

Please send the following books
I understand that I may return any book for a full refund.

❏ *Carrying the Cross to Columbine* by Garlin Newton, 160 pp., paper, $10.99

❏ *Songs of Zion* by Larry L. Colbert, 448 pp., hardback, $23.99

❏ *Unhandcuffing God* by Howard Caver, 160 pp., paper, $10.99

❏ *Dance Before the Lord* by Ron Dryden,160 pp., paper, $9.95.

❏ *33 Truths You Should Know About Jesus and the Cross* by Larry L. Colbert, 64 pp., paper, $4.95

Book Title	No. of Copies	Subtotal

Sales tax: Oklahoma residents please add 7.5%

Shipping: Free

TOTAL

Payment:
Check/money order ❏ VISA ❏ Mastercard ❏ American Express

Card Number

Name on Card   Exp. date

Name

Address

City   State   Zip

Phone

Thank you for your order!